CREATING RUGS AND WALL HANGINGS

Also by Shirley Marein

OFF THE LOOM
STITCHERY, NEEDLEPOINT, APPLIQUE AND PATCHWORK

CREATING
RUGS and WALL HANGINGS

A Complete Guide

SHIRLEY
MAREIN

RENDERINGS by ELEANOR BELLO
PHOTOGRAPHS by ALAN SWEETMAN

A STUDIO BOOK
The Viking Press NEW YORK

ACKNOWLEDGMENTS

I deeply appreciate the open generosity displayed by friends who so graciously contributed examples used in this book. My sincerest thanks to Helen Jacoff, Michael Silbert, Shirley Geller, Kitty Sadock, Sue Vanderwoude, Vera and Kenneth Maas, Syril Frank, Belle Kicinski, Lee Amsterdam, Tina Savuto, Barry Seelig, and especially to Theda Sadock for helping me locate many of the examples. The kindness of Edward Jamgotchian in sharing with me his considerable knowledge and in making available selections from his personal collection was invaluable. A grateful thank-you to Edith Karlin, Jan Silberstein, Vickie Hellmann, Janna Mandel, and Eleanor Bello for making some of the samples, and, once again, an appreciation of my two wonderful assistants, Eleanor Bello, artist, and Alan Sweetman, photographer.

Designed by Shirley and Edmund Marein

CONTENTS

To the memory of my father, who lived his
life as a patient craftsman

THERE ARE SOME ART OBJECTS so highly prized and coveted that they have become inextricably woven into the fiber of the lives of the peoples who produce them, and of those who desire them. Centuries of invasion, conquest, and foreign domination in both ancient and contemporary cultures resulted in periods of extensive migration, thus perpetuating, influencing, and expanding the development of the arts. The arts flourish during periods of calm and are always carefully protected at the first signs of unrest. There are documented references to the art of carpetmaking thousands of years old. Cherished floor coverings and wall hangings have been preserved from generation to generation in the homes of rich and poor alike, in temples and mosques, and as decoration or for other-world comfort in burial tombs, only to be later unearthed to serve again as segments in the reconstruction of past civilizations.

INTRO-DUCTION

Museum curators and archaeologists are divided in their opinions about the specific areas in which carpets and hangings may have originated, and their views are quite speculative. The Egyptians have been credited with the invention of carpetmaking, as have the Chinese. No doubt the Paracas Indians of South America, as highly skilled as other peoples in the manipulation of looms or other tensioning devices, also created carpets. Probably as the need arose, the processes for implementation were explored by widely separated peoples who had no contact with each other but had developed an adequate technical knowledge through the use of their natural resources.

It has been said that carpets were developed by nomadic tent dwellers to cover earthen floors. Animal skins may have been used at times for this purpose, but it is more than likely that tufts of hairs cut or plucked from the animals' coats and secured in woven fibers were more practical and provided softer coverings. In addition, this use led to the preservation and improvement of valuable domesticated herds, as the hunting of wild animals by primitive means requires great skill and is at best a hit-or-miss affair. Some scholars theorize that early mosaics inspired the making of carpets as tent decorations. Others feel that the carpet satisfied the need for a playing surface for games. It is a likely conjecture that the geometric quality of some designs probably did result from an admiration of mosaic flooring.

Peoples in warm climates traditionally have woven mats of reeds and bamboo fiber. In areas where the coconut abounds, the fiber surrounding the fruit has been used for weaving floor coverings. Unfortunately, dampness and humidity are destructive, and a great many of the artifacts from countries in the tropics disappeared in time, leaving no record.

Detail of Chinese rug. Collection Edward Jamgotchian

WOVEN RUGS

THE RENOWNED PILE RUGS of eastern Asia have survived from antiquity for a variety of reasons. The napped surfaces assured longevity, precious fibers such as wool and silk contributed to their value, and they were treasured for their magnitude of purpose and grandeur of scale. The admiration of the Western world for the Oriental rug has conferred universal status and lasting popularity upon the pile rug.

It is quite likely that the flat-woven or kilim rug preceded the pile rug in history. However, its diverse use as tent decoration (doubling on cold nights as a blanket for warmth), as a horse blanket and saddle cover, and in a variety of multipurpose carrying bags, confined its production to items needed locally for utilitarian purposes. The simplicity and practicality of the flat-woven rug limited its value as an export item. As a result the integrity of the designs was maintained and the continuity of those characteristic of individual villages was assured. There is a similarity between flat-woven rugs and pile rugs from the same areas because they had in common the same methods of coloring and dying wool, as well as the same traditional design elements. Pinpointing designs belonging to specific groups of people according to geographical location is difficult; political boundaries change and nomadic and semi-nomadic peoples drifted from one locale to another. One thing is certain: whether the subject matter is exotic birds of fantasy, geometric patterns, or floral motifs, the designs, whatever their significance, tend to appear geometrically angular, due to the nature of the medium. To dismiss summarily most rug designs as just "more geometric arrangements" is a mistake. The original patterns, designs, and symbols were intensely personal expressions of the thoughts and feelings of the people. Each day in the lives of ancient peoples was one of resolute triumph in dealing successfully with the natural elements: the sun and the moon, fire and water, the sea and its tides—all the harsh factors that affected human productivity, the earth's fruitfulness, and the general well-being of the individual. The worship, deification, or simple personification of these elements determined many of the designs. However, not all religions permitted representation of animal or human form, and therefore many of the designs were confined to symbolic forms. Many of the border patterns are actually decorative representations of leaves, flowers, and scrolls, designed to enclose central areas. The large background fields of design are easily identified motifs, mostly of Persian derivation. Most usual is the octagonal medallion

Prayer rug. Collection Syril Frank

known as the gul, the Persian word for rose found on Bokhara carpets. Many versions of the gul are used, the differences in interpretation depending upon the area in which the carpet was woven. The boteh motif also comes in many forms, variously described as almond shaped, teardrop shaped, or pear shaped. This design form is composed of tightly packed motifs of leaves and flowers enclosed in a geometric or scrolled border. The design occurring most frequently in Oriental carpets is the Herati motif, named for the city of Herat. It is composed of a central rosette enclosed in a diamond shape. Often the design is complicated with more rosettes placed at the points of the diamond, and leaves spaced along the straight sides. Decorative designs are numerous and have been named for places of origin, for dignitaries, or may be merely descriptive. Prayer rugs are easily recognizable by the clear forms of arches, repeating the architectural outlines of mosques and temples as shown on pages 10 and 14. The specific shapes often denote the group, the area, or the class to which the owner belonged. The rugs of Sehna have lent their names to knots still much used in rugmaking.

Color is both an important part of the emotional impact of all Oriental rugs and a major technical achievement. The beauty of the finished rug in large measure can be attributed to the skills of the people entrusted with the dyeing of the yarns. Knowledge of natural dye materials was passed from father to son, for generation after generation, as a specialized and highly esteemed art. Before the general advent of commercial aniline dyes right after World War I, when the German monopoly in the field was broken, most coloring matter was derived from vegetable material or insects. The rich ultramarine blue used in Oriental rugs was a distillation made from the leaves of the indigo plant (genus *Indigofera*). A modestly satisfactory red was obtained from the roots of the madder plant (*Rubia tinctorum*), but cochineal (*Coccus ilicis* or *Coccus cacti*), which is derived from the dried and powdered bodies of small female insects,

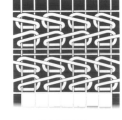

SLIT TAPESTRY

SOUMAK

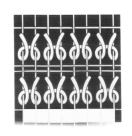

GHIORDES KNOT

GHIORDES KNOT

TYPICAL CAUCASIAN MOTIF

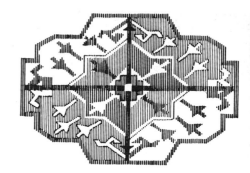

GUL

produces a fast dye that is stronger and infinitely more effective. Both have been in use since ancient times. Yellow dyes are easily made from many natural sources. A great many plants produce a straw- or ochre-colored dye. The sumac plant is most commonly used and is abundant all over the world, although the most beautiful yellow is obtained from saffron. Saffron is a flavoring as well as a dye and is obtained from the orange-colored stigmas of the garden crocus (*Crocus sativus*). Thousands of the tiny stigmas are required for the production of one ounce of saffron. These are the sources of the primary colors. Almost all the rest of the colors in the spectrum can be arrived at through mixing and blending these colors with each other in certain proportions. Oak galls, henna leaves, iron rust, barks, and hulls produce a variety of grays and browns for subduing bright colors and for providing materials for dark areas of a design.

A mordant is applied to the undyed wool to increase its receptivity to the dye and to influence its color. The most common mordant used was alum (potassium aluminum sulfate). It does not make the color fast. Most vegetable materials contain tannic acid, and this is an aid to colorfastness. When tannic acid is not present, or present only in small quantities, additions of acetic acid (in the form of vinegar) or uric acid were used. Antique rugs are mellowed by sun, exposure to light, and cleaning, which produce even tonal values and great softness and beauty in the natural coloring.

Since abundant natural resources inspire and suggest the undertaking of specific crafts, continued experimentation is devoted to the perfection and development of native materials in all cultures. It can also be assumed that the evolution of indigenous arts in settled cultures will start simply but will eventually result in complex techniques. Just as stone masonry and sculpture reached perfection in areas where the materials were plentiful, and wood carving and wood construction developed in heavily forested regions, so the greatest weaving traditions naturally arose where the resources were sufficient to the needs. Great plateaus of pasture land stretching through Asia Minor, Persia, Afghanistan, and Turkestan were natural habitats for sheep and easily provided proper nourishment for the production of fine fleece. Abraham was a shepherd, following one of the earliest occupations mentioned in the Bible.

GUL

GUL

BOTEH

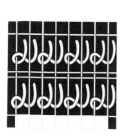

SEHNA KNOT

SEHNA KNOT

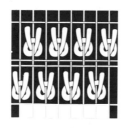

SPANISH KNOT

11

Until the development of chemical fibers, the wool of sheep constituted almost half of the warp and weft threads of all rugs and about 90 per cent of the rug pile used on knotted rugs. Silk, cotton, linen, jute, and various types of animal hair, such as that of the camel, yak, and goat, and human hair as well, made up the difference. The fleece of sheep is preferable because, due to its structure, it is easily spun and is flexible when knotted. The natural colors of sheep wool subtly adapt to dyes, and its composition accepts and holds the dyes more readily than other types of fiber.

Although excavations have not revealed actual examples of carpets from the Greek and Roman eras, there are references in literature to Greek and Roman admiration for Eastern carpets and wall hangings. The earliest known carpet was excavated by the Russians, in an excellent state of preservation, from the ice in a Scythian burial mount at Pazryck near the border of Outer Mongolia. The 6' × 6' Pazryck carpet, threadbare but with recognizable motifs of horses and deer, has been dated by radioactive carbon tests as being from the fifth century B.C. Because the workmanship is quite delicate and extremely sophisticated (225 knots per square inch) it is thought that the carpet might be of Eastern origin.

There is a great deal of speculation about Roman activities in this field. Roman trade and communications with the East were extensive. No doubt the Romans were fully aware of the superior quality of the fine wools used in Oriental carpets and improved their own and Asian stock by interbreeding. Over the centuries the Romans expanded their empire, colonizing large areas of Egypt, North Africa, and Western Europe. Everything necessary to the positive establishment of the Roman Empire in distant, relatively uncultivated, un-

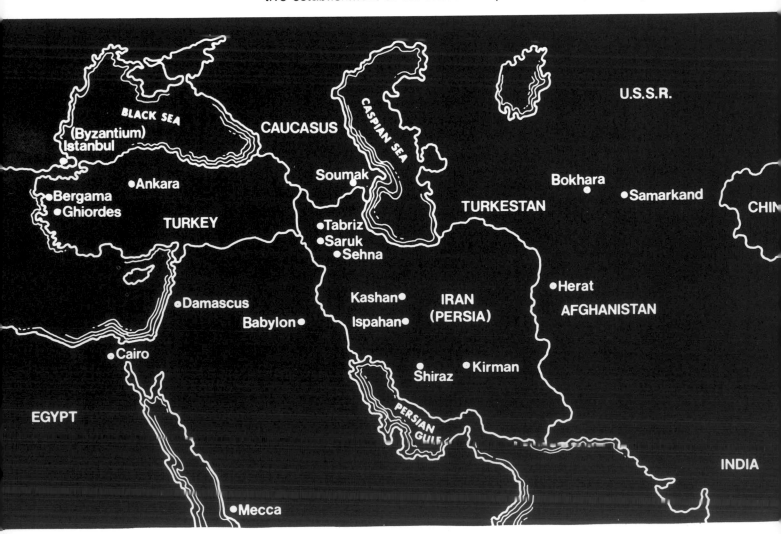

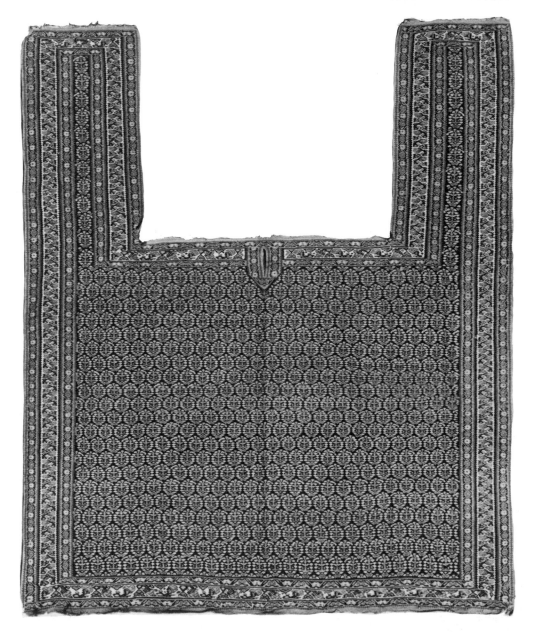

Flat-woven Sehna horse blanket with boteh designs. Collection Edward Jamgotchian

civilized areas was brought with them, including families of experienced craftsmen, their tools, and herds of domesticated animals. The sheep accompanying the Romans on their conquests were probably the antecedents of the celebrated Spanish Merino herds.

The handful of Arab and Berber troops who later crossed the Straits of Gibraltar from North Africa to the Iberian peninsula proved a most powerful force in the development of the textile industry in western Europe. With the Arab arrival in A.D. 711, the domination of Spain by the Visigoths was ended, and most of the peninsula flourished under Muslim rule during the next eight centuries. In southern Spain, with centers in Cordova and Granada, the Islamic dynasties developed a civilization of unprecedented brilliance. The Muslims permitted a cultural atmosphere in which they, the Christians, and the Jews coexisted, and they easily assimilated the forms of classical antiquity and of the Far East, adding them to their own Middle Eastern background. Spain was noted for its wool and linen textiles before the Islamic conquest; afterward it became a renowned center for silk weaving. Somewhat later the manufacture of rugs is mentioned in literature, and the findings of early fragments revealed that they were pile rugs. In all cases a knot is wrapped around a single warp, forming a loop which is then cut. Flat-woven rugs are rare, although the peninsula is noted for embroidered rugs and wall hangings made on a plain-weave linen canvas.

Prayer rug. Collection Michael Silbert

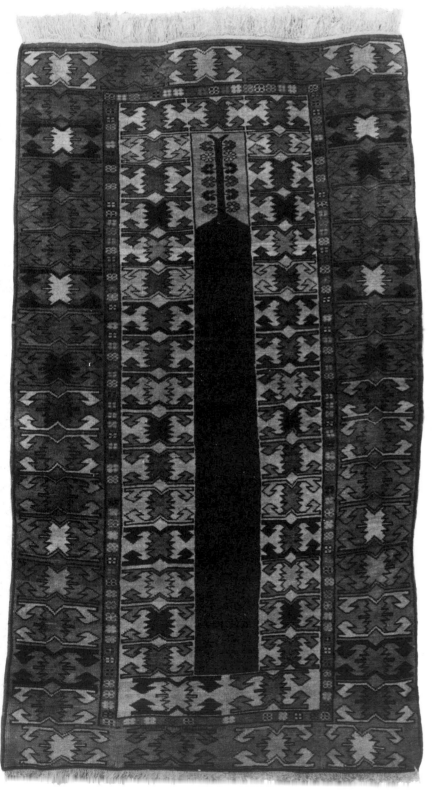

TRADITIONAL BORDER DESIGNS

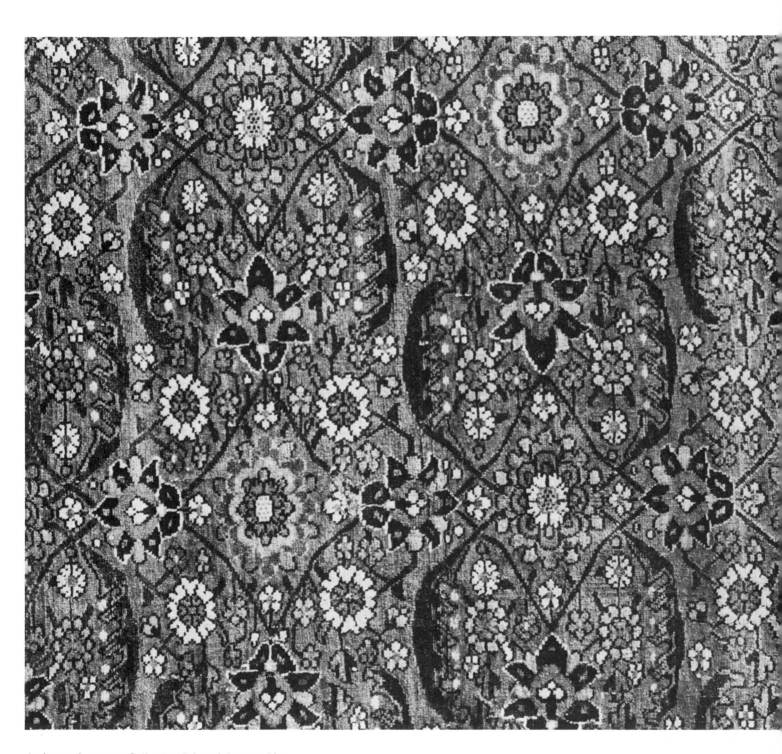

Joshegan fragment. Collection Edward Jamgotchian

Before the arrival of the Spanish in North America during the sixteenth and seventeenth centuries, a weaving tradition existed among the Pueblo men of the southwestern United States and the Tlingit women of the northwest Pacific coastal region. Wild bighorn sheep with very coarse coats are native to the Rocky Mountains, as are the mountain goats of the Northwest, and these could supply the materials that were necessary for weaving warm blankets and clothing. The ingenious Tlingits of southeastern Alaska processed the bark of the giant red cedars and utilized it for weaving mats. These mats served as wall coverings, insulating the cedar plank walls of their large and drafty communal homes, which often measured 40′ × 50′. With further refinement, the cedar bark was usable to make warp strings for their looms and, in combination with mountain goat hair, for weaving. Vertical warp-weighted looms without heddles were used by the Chilkat Indians, an Alaskan Tlingit tribe from the Chilkat River area, weavers of a particularly spectacular cape blanket. Since a loom without heddles does not provide for opening a shed to allow the weft to pass through, the Chilkat blankets are twined in a flat-woven tapestry technique. The designs, similar to those of the totem poles of the area, are of family crests and family legends worked in a traditional color scheme of green, black, yellow, and white. Although it is the usual Indian practice to create designs without

CHARACTERISTIC NAVAJO PATTERNS

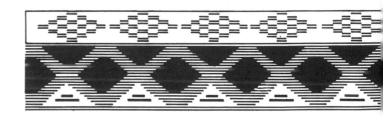

Navajo rug from the Teec Nos Pos area. Collection Dr. and Mrs. Theodore R. Sadock

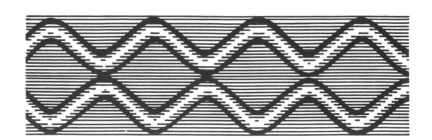

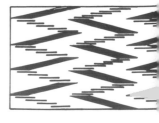

drawn patterns, these weavers were women, and as the woman in Indian culture may not originate designs based on life forms, the designs were drawn on boards by men and copied by the women weavers.

In South America the pre-Columbian textiles woven by the coastal Indians of the Peruvian area are at least comparable and sometimes are thought superior to those of the same period in Europe, parts of Asia, and India. Many kinds of fiber of excellent quality were easily available. Wool was supplied by the llama, the domesticated alpaca, and the wild vicuña, which is treasured for its very fine and remarkably silky hair. The climate of Peru was well suited to producing cotton that had a natural brown-and-white cotton fiber. Even, tightly twisted spinning was accomplished by hand without the aid of a spindle. Exceptional weaves were achieved on a backstrap loom that had heddles for opening a shed. It is more than likely that two or more sets of heddles were used for intricate patterns. Excavations have unearthed textiles still in a remarkable state of preservation, due to the dryness of the sandy burial sites. However, with the exception of easily identified clothing, there is only supposition as to the precise use of most Peruvian textiles. None can be claimed with any certainty to have been used as carpets, although many of the fragments and flat pieces exhibit looping and highly perfected tapestry techniques.

Spanish explorers introduced horses and other domesticated animals, including sheep, to the Americas. Inventories list thousands of sheep accompanying governors sent from Spain to settle the southwestern territories of the United States. During the ensuing periods of dissension and wars many of the

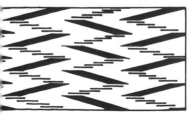

Fragment of a Paracas textile. Collection of the author

Pueblo Indians were subjugated or lost their lives to raiding tribes and the determined Spanish. Others fled, joining the stronger, more independent Navajos. Eventually, through proximity and intermarriage, significant elements of Pueblo development were absorbed into the Navajo culture. During the long period of assimilation between the community-minded Pueblos and the warlike Navajos both tribes benefited from the agricultural methods and the wondrous new animals brought by the Spanish. The weaving skills of the Pueblo men became the province of the Navajo women as the Navajo men proved better suited to their accustomed roles as hunters and warriors. In time sheep raising became the foundation of Navajo community life.

After a short period of imitating the designs of the Pueblos, Navajo women soon developed a style of their own. The earliest late-eighteenth and early-nineteenth century fragments, found in caves that had been abandoned after a massacre, are made in striped patterns of coarsely hand-spun, undyed wool in shades of natural white and brown. Smaller fragments of this period are finer in weave, due to the use of unraveled yarn from cloth brought by the Spaniards. English baize (called bayeta in Spanish) is a coarse woolen fabric having a relatively long nap. It is the type of flannel often used on card or billiard tables. This particular cloth, preferably in red, was shipped from Spain and used as a trade item among both the Pueblos and the Navajos. The Navajos cut it into strips, unraveled it, and twisted the strands together in the manner of spinning. Sometimes the unraveled strands were carded and then respun. Early bayeta flannel fabric was dyed red with cochineal; later American flannel used for unraveling was of lesser quality. Aniline-dyed fibers used in early Navajo blankets can be distinguished by their red-orange color. It is curious that natural dyes were rarely used by Navajo weavers before the present-day enthusiasm for vegetable dyeing. Indigo from Mexico was introduced by the Spanish and accounted for the occasional blue stripe of the early period. With the introduction of three-ply Saxony yarn from Germany and four-ply Germantown yarn from Pennsylvania, a greater variety of colors, in addition to softer textures, widened the range of the weaver. A single blanket might employ undyed hand-spun native yarn, aniline-dyed hand-spun yarn, unraveled bayeta, and three- or four-ply commercial yarn.

A parallel can be drawn between the concepts of contemporary artists and the early Navajo designers to the extent that in both cases the shapes are broad and density is achieved without depth. Scale is particularly interesting in Navajo rugs; the simplicity of striping, both narrow and broad, contributes a feeling of great size. A later development in Navajo design was the use of undulating stripes, rising and falling peaks, and closed diamonds. The intense color and strength of the new aniline dyes, more apparent when used in alternating stripes, created a dazzling vibrancy in the later rugs.

In recorded history there is no evidence that the Indians of North America used anything other than an upright loom, rather than the backstrap loom of the Indians of Mexico and South America. A rough frame was constructed by pounding vertical posts into the ground and lashing horizontal bars to the top and bottom to form an upright rectangle. On these looms warping is done on two bars laid parallel to the ground. After warping, the bars are fastened to the upright frame. When the weaver seated on the ground in front of the loom can no longer comfortably reach the portion in progress, the bars holding the warp are lowered on the rough frame and retied. The finished portion is rolled or folded up and sewn tightly to itself, and the ends of the warping bar are lashed to the horizontal bar at the bottom of the rough frame. The rough frame is adjusted to the desired size of each new blanket. A continuous heddle lifts alternate threads, opening a shed across the width of the warp. Navajo blankets are characteristically four-selvage. They are twined at the bottom of the warping bar; the bar is then removed and the twined area lashed to the bar. Each blanket is woven to the very end of the warp. As weaving becomes more difficult and the shed can no longer be opened with the heddling device, the weft is inserted by hand with a long needle. Another distinctive feature of the Navajo blanket is the braided appearance of the sides. The edges are strengthened with a tightly plied cord added alongside the end warp strings, woven with the weft and twisted around the end warp about every half inch.

Green-corn-and-rainbow yei figure on a Navajo pillow top from the Lukachukai area. Collection Dr. and Mrs. Theodore R. Sadock

Navajo blankets were used for warmth—as an outer wrap, for sitting or sleeping on the ground, or as a door covering, never as a rug. With the coming of the railroad to the West, the Navajo blanket became a major trade item. As the settlers, ranchers, military men, and cowboys did not need to use Navajo blankets as clothing, the size increased to cover the conventional bed, and assorted throws were made as rugs and decorative wall hangings.

Two Gray Hills area Navajo rug. Collection Dr. and Mrs. Theodore R. Sadock

Flat-woven kilim rug. Collection Michael Silbert

THERE ARE MANY TYPES OF construction methods to choose from for weaving flat and textured rugs and wall hangings without a high pile. Of all fiber constructions, the two-element method of twining or twisting two or more weft threads together around each warp is the most solid and durable. Twining is especially suitable for mats and small rugs.

The basic weave used in the largest proportion of all textile work is the traditional plain weave, familiarly called tabby. Even distribution of warp and weft threads worked alternately over and under, over and under each other from selvage to selvage in the manner of darning will produce a firm, reversible plain-weave fabric. Variations can be made with color changes and by the use of different fiber textures. Very early, possibly in prehistoric times, an impatient weaver worked the weft thread over two and under two warp threads and invented the basket weave. An extension of the basket weave is the rep or flat weave, in which the warp and the weft threads extend over and under each other unequally. Brocading varies the plain weave by superimposing or laying in an additional weft thread for pattern or color emphasis. The supplementary thread is wound into a butterfly, the end inserted in the shed at any point, along with the weft thread, creating designs that may stop or may be carried up into the next row.

Fragment of a Coptic fabric. Collection Leon Pomerance

Tapestry is a decorative method of painting with yarn. The plain-weave technique consists of color areas freely woven in, to butt each other at random and rise irregularly on the warp. Individual butterflies of different-colored yarns are made up, and the yarn is woven back and forth in the sheds without going from selvage to selvage. The yarn is tightly beaten down on the warp until the warp is entirely invisible. The colored yarns may be linked to each other or woven back and forth without linking, causing a slit to form in the fabric. The slit may be sewn together or remain open as a frank structural occurrence inherent in the technique.

Soumak and chaining add texture to the plain-weave surface and could be considered a way to add a low pile when used in conjunction with a plain weave. Both forms will rise above the plain weave, producing a ridge that becomes more pronounced with a change in the weight of the yarn. Both stitches are woven on a closed shed but require the opening of the shed for the plain weaving necessary to hold them in place and produce a sturdy fabric.

21

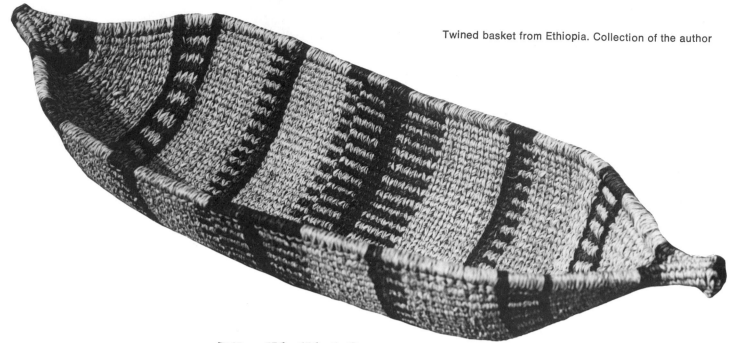

TWINING

SINCE A CONTAINER IS NECESSARY to hold a store of corn or berries, the earliest woven form was possibly a basket. A practical approach to the problem of holding reeds together is to twine one to another with dried grasses. Among primitive people simple twining preceded the advanced processes of carding and spinning essential to the production of a pliable fiber for weaving softer, finer fabrics. The Tlingit Indians produced baskets so tightly woven that they could hold water and be used as cooking utensils. Hot stones held with wooden tongs were dropped on meat or fish placed in the basket, and sufficient water was added to generate steam; then the basket was covered until the food was cooked. The technique of twining was used by the Indians to make fish nets, to construct huge mats for use as canoe sails and as floor coverings for the interior of the canoe as well as for their dwellings, to make cradles, and to weave winding-sheets. Lengths of root from spruce trees, varying from 3′ to 20′ long, and occasionally much longer, were dug from under the trees and used, after preparation and curing, for both warp and weft. Stems of grasses wrapped around the outside weft, in the manner of embroidery, provided decoration. The grasses were often dyed to provide a complement to the natural creamy color of the spruce roots.

MATERIALS

Today twining materials may include almost any fiber or fabric, synthetic or natural, that is reasonably pliable. Some mats are made of reeds, raffia, sisal, and coconut fibers. Many of these tough, brittle fibers are made pliable, and therefore easier to manipulate, by soaking.

In twining, warp strings must be strong and sturdy to minimize breaking during the weaving process. If the warp is to be entirely covered by the weft, its color is not a consideration. A fringe of neutral-colored warp strings is structural. A contrasting fringe could be added after the weaving has been completed. Heavyweight linen and cotton warping thread is serviceable and suitable for rugs. Jute twine, three-ply or heavier, is excellent. Two- and three-ply wool may also be used for warping. Sisal is somewhat difficult to work with because of its rugged texture. The weft will not move up and down easily over rough sisal with short, protruding fibers. These short fibers may also come through and appear on the surface of the weft. This particular type of surface, however, is often desirable for an outdoor mat. The weft may be of one material or a combination of materials that are of approximately the same weight. Weft twining automatically spaces the warp, and a very thin and very thick combination will cause a variation in the width of the finished piece. A very thin fiber can be utilized doubled, although the possibility of tangles will be great. Thin woolen fibers can be plied. The plying of two contrasting colors contributes a decorative note, but plying all of the weft is time-consuming. Rug yarns of two and three ply work well, as do jute, sisal, and cable cord. New or used tricot, woolen, and cotton fabrics, cut in long strips for twining, are effective in a rural atmosphere. For a more sophisticated setting, strips of leather or vinyl might be used.

GLOSSARY

WARP
Spaced parallel threads running vertically.

TWINING WEFT
Horizontal threads enclosing the warp.

BEATER
Tool for compacting the weft by pressing it down between warps.

PLY
Two or more strands of yarn twisted together to form a single strand.

SQUARE KNOT
A sturdy knot, made with two ends, that will not open under tension.

TO LAY IN YARN
Method of introducing new, additional weft yarn.

HALF TWIST
One weft crosses over another between each two warps.

FULL TWIST
One weft crosses over another, completing a full turn between each two warps.

PAIRED TWINING
One weft crosses over another between pairs of warps.

LOOPED TWINING
One of two wefts is pulled forward in a loop.

BUTTERFLY
Yarn wound up to shorten length.

Twining is easily worked on a rigid warp. Tie the warp at both top and bottom to horizontal bars or wind it continuously around the bars. The Indians worked the weft by pushing upward on a warp hanging free at the bottom and attached at the top to a holding cord supported by upright poles. If the holding cord is looped in a complete circle around the upright supports, the weft can be woven in the round to make a bag or basket. The free-hanging warp is attached to the holding cord with a lark's head (reverse double half hitch) knot (see page 212).

CONSTRUCTING A FRAME TO HOLD THE WARP

The weight of the lumber used for construction of a frame is in direct relationship to its length and width. Artists' stretcher strips are suitable for a small frame. Stretcher strip sizes up to 30″ will hold their rigidity without warping out of shape. Because the wood in stretcher strips is rather thin, larger-size frames should be constructed of heavier lumber. For instance, ¾″ × 1¾″ is more practical for any size over 30″. A 5′ frame requires 2″ × 2″ lumber.

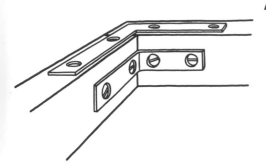

ASSEMBLING THE FRAME

A. Stretcher Strips

1. Apply glue to the slim, protruding tabs. Insert the tabs into the accommodating slots alongside them.
2. Hammer corners into place. Make certain the sides are parallel to each other and the corners are at right angles before the glue dries.
3. For more security, place a screw of appropriate length in each corner, securing the front, the tab, and the back of the stretcher strips.

B. A Frame of Heavier Lumber

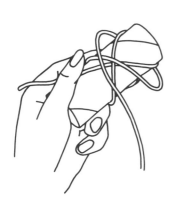

1. Have lumber cut to the desired size. The top and bottom horizontal lengths must extend across the vertical sides. The top bar will rest on the side bars, and the side bars on top of the bottom bar.
2. Arrange the frame on the floor or on a workbench.
3. Place angle irons in the corners.
4. Mark the position of the screws on the wood by drawing a pencil line around each hole in the iron.
5. Use a hand drill with a bit smaller than the screw size to make an opening for the screw. A starting hole may also be made with an awl and hammer if a drill is not available.
6. Replace the angle irons and secure the screws in each hole.
7. To correct movement or play in a large frame, screw flat L-shaped angles to the surface of each corner of the frame.

Winding yarn on a tube (above) and with a mechanical winder (below)

WARPING THE FRAME

Decide in advance whether a fringe will be practical to make and suitable to both the design of the finished piece and the situation in which it will be used. The alternative to fringed ends is a four-selvage weave. Should a four-selvage weave be elected, a fringe may still be added after the rug is completed. The question of whether or not you want the woven piece to be finished with a selvage on all four sides must be decided before you begin warping. Two selvages can be accomplished by warping directly onto a rigid frame. To make four selvages, the warp must be wound around bars that are supported by the frame but can be removed when the weaving is near completion.

Hanking yarn on a swift

When the warp is placed around the upper and lower bars of the frame, the weaving area is automatically limited to the space between the bars. The unusable warp around the top and bottom bars becomes a simple fringe. More elaborate fringes can be worked if longer lengths of warp are left unwoven. Warp the frame in figure eights as explained below. A continuous warp is most satisfactory because it is one without breaks and knots on the workable surface. (If a break occurs in the warping thread, or the thread has run out and an addition is necessary, cut the thread at least 3″ or 4″ from the top or bottom of the frame. Attach the new thread to the cut extension with a square knot. Tighten the knot against the outside center of the bar where it can be cut off later.)

Start the warping at the bottom of the frame about 3″ or 4″ from the side bar. Always allow several inches of free space on either side between warp and frame to allow for easy manipulation of the weft with the hands.

WINDING THE WARP IN FIGURE EIGHTS

Wind the end of the warp around the bottom bar several times and knot it to itself with a square knot. The knot will eventually be cut off and the end will become part of the fringe. Bring the warp up to the top of the frame, over and around the bar, down to the bottom, over and around the bottom bar in a figure eight. Repeat until enough double-warp turns have been completed to make the work the desired width. Weft twining spaces the warp threads about 1/4" apart. A warp of strong two-ply rug yarn will space out, after twining, to about 6 threads per inch; therefore 48 warp turns around the back and front result in a surface of 96 single warp ends. After twining, the width will be approximately 16". A finer warp and weft will have a narrower finished width and require additional warping to make wider widths. Heavier warping materials with larger circumferences, such as jute and sisal, produce wider widths with less warp ends per inch. Complete the warping on the lower bar, opposite the starting point, for an even count. Wrap the end around the lower bar several times and tie it with a square knot. Warp firmly with even tension, without

Twining on a frame loom

25

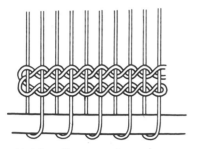
Twining the warp to make a selvage

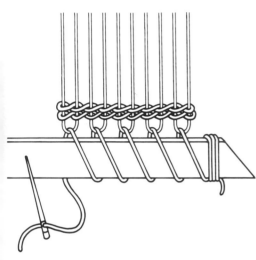
Whipping the warp to the stretcher bar

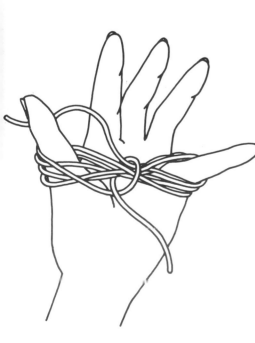

slack, but also without stretching the yarn. Warp wound in figure eights will produce a shed (or cross) in the warp threads. Although no shed is necessary in twining, the figure-eight warping helps to keep the warp ends separate and in order. It does not affect the appearance of the finished piece. Place the flat of your hand in the space between the threads, move it up or down, and feel the crossing of the threads. Place a dowel or a narrow piece of lath as wide as the warp in the opening between the front and back warp, above the point where they cross, and pull the stick down toward the bottom bar. It will stop comfortably about an inch from the top of the bottom bar. The stick will take up any slight slack in the warp and act as a straight horizontal guide for the first row of twining. After the weaving has been completed, or if the warp becomes too taut at any time during the weaving, remove the stick.

MAKING FOUR SELVAGES

To produce a smoothly finished, fringeless edge at top and bottom, the warp must be wound in a figure eight around removable bars supported on a frame. For easy removal, smooth, round dowels or poles are best. The dowels, suspended from the top and bottom of the frame with sufficient room between dowel and frame for easy passage of the ball of warp, are removed after the first two rows of twining are done. To place the dowels exactly, measure down from the top of the frame and hammer 2″ nails into the side bars. Allow the nails to protrude approximately 1″. Place the frame on a flat surface, positioning the dowels against the nails, on the sides nearest the end bars. Tie each dowel to the side bars with twine. The span between the dowels will be the approximate finished length of the woven piece. As the warp must be continuous and of even tension, allow sufficient time to complete the warping in one session.

Draw the warp end around the bottom dowel. Bring the end up on itself about 3″ and fasten it with a square knot. Draw the warp up and over the opposite dowel and down again and over the bottom dowel, forming a figure eight. Complete the warping, finishing on the opposite end of the beginning dowel. Bring the end up several inches and tie a knot on the last warp thread.

Twine two rows of weft through the warp, using the half turn. Remove the dowel and carefully push the twining down to the ends of the warp turns. Using strong linen thread, whip each warp turn to the stretcher bar.

PREPARING THE WEFT FOR TWINING

Because twining encircles the warp, enclosing it completely from both sides, the weft is used doubled over on itself so that one half may go behind the warp as the other comes in front. Select the yarn and cut a four-yard length. Bring the cut ends together evenly. Mark the center of the length with a short string of contrasting color. Shorten both ends to workable length by winding each end into a butterfly.

TO MAKE A BUTTERFLY

The butterfly winds up long lengths of yarn so that it will pull out as needed without tangling and becoming knotted. Doubled-over yarn arranged for twining is started a workable distance (about 12″) away from the center marker. Hold your hand up, palm facing you, with fingers spread apart. Drop the portion of yarn to be wound over the palm and between the thumb and index finger, allowing the 12″ to the marker and the other half of the yarn to hang loosely behind the palm of the hand.

For a single butterfly, place a ball of yarn in a bowl at your feet and drop the cut end of the yarn between the thumb and index finger. Allow about 8″ to hang loosely behind the palm of your hand. Spread your thumb and pinkie comfortably apart. Bring the yarn resting on your palm around the outside of the pinkie, through the space between the pinkie and the next finger. Draw the yarn toward you, across the palm, and around the outside of the thumb, around the thumb, across the palm, and around the outside of the pinkie again in a figure eight. A butterfly containing two, three, or four yards is workable. Too much yarn wound in this fashion has a tendency to become disorganized before the quantity is used. When about 12″ remains after winding, end the butterfly over and around the thumb. Holding the fingers out taut, draw the yarn down with the other hand and push the end under the center of the entire butterfly. Pull the end loosely over the top and insert it through the loose loop left from the last turn around the thumb. Pull the end firmly. Draw the end up again through the center of the butterfly loosely, pulling the end through the loop to secure it. Remove the butterfly from the fingers. The yarn will pull out easily, without knotting, when pulled from the end that was left hanging over the back of your hand.

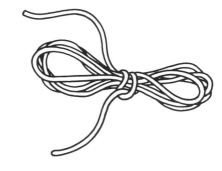

WEFT TWINING

The doubled-over weft, one strand coming from behind the warp thread and the other crossing in front of it, encloses each warp thread or group of warp threads. All variations in texture and pattern stem from different combinations of the basic technique of encircling the warp. Try various combinations by making a sampler mat or small wall hanging. Twine around one warp at a time with a half turn, or twist, of the weft yarn between each warp, enclose two warps at a time, or alternate—one and two, one and two—for a different effect. A full turn of the weft between warps changes the width and the appearance of the weaving, as does the combination of two colors. There are many possible choices. Wall hangings can also be made without parallel selvages, by using weft yarns that are longer than the width of the warp and weaving them in one direction only, allowing the wefts to protrude just beyond the warp or to hang down at either or both sides.

In continuous weaving, the turning back at the end of each row can be done by either of two methods: In the *plain turn* the crossing is reversed on the return row so that both rows will look the same. In the *countered turn* twists cross away from each other on each successive row. When each row of twining runs in the opposite direction to the previous row, the appearance is that of an upright zigzag instead of the straight lines produced by the plain turn. Changes and alternations in these turns at the end of the row, and in the half and full turns of the weft that can be made between individual warp threads or pairs of threads, make possible a great variety of pattern.

WEAVING

The first row of twining spaces the warp. Start the basic weaving from the bottom and work upward, but remember to place a single row of twining across the top of the warp to keep the warp strings in place. End the single top row by tying the excess at the end of the row to the top frame bar. Begin from either side of the warp by placing the marker of the doubled-over weft outside of the first warp thread. Draw half the weft from behind the first warp, pulling it forward and allowing it to remain in that position. The other half of the weft crosses the first warp in the front. Slip it under the second warp and bring it forward. Pick up the first weft again and pass it under the third warp, bringing it forward. Pick up the weft coming from behind the second warp, cross in front of the third warp, and pass it under the fourth warp. When the doubled-over yarn is woven to enclose a warp, one section going over and the other section going under the warp, it is easy to produce a thick, reversible, and extremely durable mat. The half turn, sometimes called a half twist, is the basic structure of twining. The width of the woven piece can be expanded by using a full turn, or full twist, between warps. Twining over two warp strings at one time is faster and will decrease the finished width somewhat.

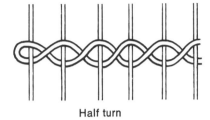

Half turn

Half Turn

Two wefts, one coming from the back of the warp, the other from the front, cross each other with a *half* twist between each warp. The use of two contrasting colors, one color for the back weft and another color for the weft crossing at the front, will result in alternating color dashes.

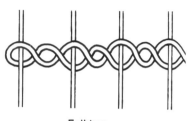

Full turn

Full Turn

Two wefts, one coming from the back of the warp, the other from the front, cross each other with a *full* twist between each warp. The full twist spaces the warp threads farther apart from each other, increasing the width of the finished piece. With the use of two colors the full twist between each warp will result in one full row of one color and a full row of another color.

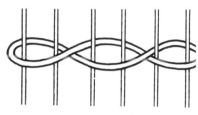

Paired twining

Paired Twining

Two wefts, one coming from the back of the warp, the other from the front, enclose two warp threads at each crossing. Each crossing can be completed with a half turn or a full turn.

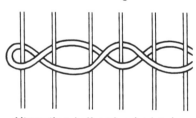

Alternating half and paired twining

Alternating Half Turns and Paired Twining

Two wefts, one from the back of the warp, the other from the front, enclose one warp thread, then two warp threads, alternating one and two warp threads across the row. Each crossing can be completed with a half turn or a full turn.

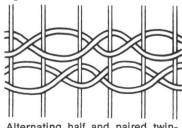

Alternating half and paired twining

Alternating Paired Twining

Another effect is achieved by moving forward one warp thread in each group of two warp threads on alternate rows.

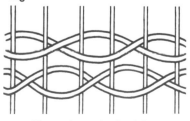

Alternating paired twining

Continuous weaving of half turns, with firm beating, will make a very thick, compact fabric. Beating (pressing down the woven rows to compact the weft) is done by inserting a tool with tines like a fork, or like a comb with widespread teeth, between the warp threads and pushing down horizontally with even pressure. The kind of turnback used at the end of a row in order to start the following row will influence the textural appearance of the weaving. Plain turning produces even, regular weaving because the wefts cross each other in the same direction in each successive row. The countered turn, easily recognizable because the result resembles knitting, will cause the weft to cross in one direction in one row and in the opposite direction in the next row. Many small patterns are possible when two colors are used. When weaving back and forth across rows, changes from plain to countered twining can easily be made in the turns at the ends of rows.

Plain Turns

1. At the end of a row, weft A passes over the last warp and turns around the warp, crossing in front of weft B as it emerges from behind the last warp. A is then placed behind the last warp to start the return across the row. Do not draw weft A forward.

2. Weft B, emerging from behind the last warp, goes over the last warp and under the second warp.

3. Weft A comes over weft B and over the second warp and then goes under warp three, to complete the turn. Continue plain twining across the row, placing the butterfly of weft above the weaving before and after each crossing. On the third row draw both wefts toward you. For even, compact twining, the wefts must cross each other in the same direction on each row; therefore the positioning of the weft must be slightly different on the return in alternate rows.

Countered Turns

1. Proceed in the same manner as the first step in Plain Turns, except that weft A, after going behind the last warp, is drawn forward toward the weaver.

2. Weft B starts back across the row by turning over the last warp and under the second warp.

3. Weft A is picked up, crosses up over weft B, goes over warp two and under warp three, completing the turn for continued twining running counter to the row below.

Some experimenting is necessary to utilize the turns successfully. The countered turn is especially useful for reversing colors in a two-colored weft.

LAYING IN NEW YARN

When the weft is near its end, make a new single butterfly of the same color. Rarely do the two wefts run out at the same time. If you want a smooth selvage on the right and left side, never start a new weft near the edges. Always stop four or five warps short of the edge and lay in a new weft. Place the pulling end of the butterfly over the old short weft end which is hanging in the front. Push the new end between the two warps from which the short weft emerges and drop a few inches of weft behind the weaving. Continue twining with the two wefts until the short one is finished. Clip ends short after the weaving is done.

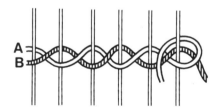

Plain turns

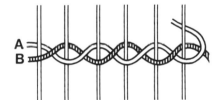

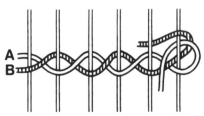

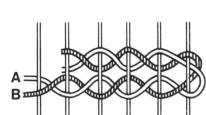

Countered turns

TWINING WITH LOOPS

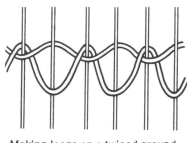

Making loops on a twined ground

Pulling down on the crossing weft of the half turn with the fingers will form a loop. Two or three rows of tightly packed plain or countered twining should follow each row of loops constructed in this fashion, to secure them. These loops will have a tendency to shift if pulled from side to side, so it is not wise to cut them in the center for a shaggy appearance. If you do want a shaggy effect, a loop can be locked into position by bringing the weft back and around to encircle the warp before proceeding under the next warp. One row of twining firmly beaten down will easily hold a secured loop in place. These secured loops can be cut in the center. Experiment with different types of yarn. A fluffy, soft yarn will give a fuller appearance; two colors will result in a tweedy effect. The length of individual loops, or rows of loops, can vary.

FINISHING

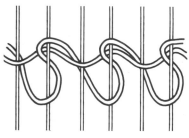

Locking the loops in position

Four-selvage weaving, when released from the holding bars, is ready for use as a rug or wall hanging. If the weaving has instead been worked around the frame, cut the warp across the center top of the frame bar with scissors or a sharp blade. Cut and finish one side at a time. The short fringe ends in small, even groups of four or six warp ends, using an overhand knot pushed up close to the weaving. Longer warp ends can be knotted in double rows of alternating square knots. Add additional fringe or fringes where there are none by attaching cut lengths of yarn to the edges with lark's head knots. Finish all loose ends on the reverse side by clipping them short or pulling them back into and through the weaving structure with a crochet hook.

Twining. Detail of warp crossing of free-hanging warp

Below: Free-hanging warp started with lark's head macramé knots

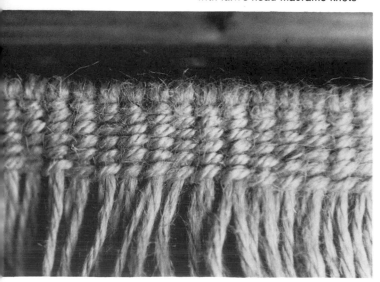

TAPESTRY

NO ONE HAS EVER BEEN ABLE to determine the origin of the tapestry weave. It has been in continuous use by all primitive peoples and was well known before the Christian era. Exactly how far back in time the interweaving of fiber may have developed is still open to speculation. Men of the Stone Age may very well have used this method of construction. Whatever its origins, the method is obviously the easiest way to hold slender fibers together in order to make a large, flat, soft, and pliable surface. The process itself is just a simple matter of lacing one set of horizontal fibers over and under another set of vertical fibers. When the horizontal fibers (the weft) are firmly packed down, the product is a fabric so firm, sturdy, and impenetrable that it will keep a room warm when it is hung on the wall, or provide a heavy, flat floor covering.

Because the basic principle of weaving one strand over and under another is so simple, it can be done without a loom. Ancient Greek weavers threw many strands of thread over a bar, weighted them at the bottom with rocks, and then wove across them, working from the top down, to make sufficient fabric for their lavishly draped clothing. However, the slowness of weaving on a warp-weighted loom can be remedied by attaching the vertical warp strands to a frame at top and bottom.

The ancient Greeks also used a holding rod and heddle. Heddles are moderately short cords attached to every other warp thread in order to separate them from the mass of threads. Instead of lacing the weft thread over and under, over and under alternate warp threads, the heddles provide a means of pulling groups of alternate threads forward in order to allow the weft to pass behind them. This basic technique is used all over the world for tapestry weaving. In the Near East flat woven tapestry rugs and hangings are called kilims; the very same technique is used by the Peruvians, the Navajos, the Mexicans, and the Central Americans, and is also characteristic of the Gobelin and Aubusson rugs and wall hangings of France.

31

Mr. Adam's Apple by Archie Brennan. Tapestry of cotton warp and wool and linen weft with assemblage of wood. Photo Tom Scott

MATERIALS

In weaving, there are so many yarns to choose from that selection and iden-tification become very confusing. "Yarn" may be spun of any natural or syn-thetic fiber and may include many strands. "Thread" usually refers either to a single filament of a synthetic material, or to a long, single strand made of fibrous materials twisted together.

All natural fibers are products of animal, vegetable, or mineral material. The most common animal fibers are spun from the wool and hair of sheep, camels, llamas, alpacas, vicuñas, cows, horses, or goats. Mohair is spun from the hair of the angora goat. Cashmere is spun from the very fine, soft hair of the Kash-mir goat. Especially fine short hairs, such as those used in cashmere fabrics, are often mixed with sturdier fibers for longer wear. Even combings from long-haired cats and dogs can be spun into a usable fiber. The silkworm is a valuable worker because the silk filament it spins need only be wound from the cocoon into skeins.

Vegetable fibers are derived from certain plants. These plants, notably flax, hemp, ramie, and jute, are sometimes referred to as bast or bast fibers, mean-ing that the fiber is of a strong and woody type. The agave family of plants, native to Mexico and Central America, produce the maguey and sisal fibers generally used to make cord. Sisal gets its name from the port known as Sisal in the Yucatán. There are other vegetable fibers, such as kapok, from the seed of the kapok tree, and piña, from the long leaves of the pineapple plant. Cotton, a plant fiber, has provided a substantial part of the world's cloth. Asbestos is a mineral fiber commonly used in making fireproof curtains and protective clothing. Gold and silver, as well as silica, the basic compound in the manu-facture of glass, are other minerals used. Synthetic fibers, however, are pro-duced by combining and spinning chemical compounds. One of the most widely used of these fibers is rayon, also a synthesis, composed mainly of cellulose compounds.

The preparation and processing of wool fiber is lengthy, consisting of cutting and sorting, scouring, blending, dyeing (either before or after spinning), and carding, spinning, and plying. A fleece from a single sheep might contain

Tapestry rug adapted from a Rufino Tamayo painting. Collection Dr. and Mrs. H. Amsterdam

fourteen grades of fiber, from the very soft, fine under hair to the coarse protective outer coat. After carding (a fine-combing process designed to eliminate burrs and tangles and tease the fibers into a soft fluffiness) the conditioned fibers, now called wool roving, are ready for spinning. Spinning is a twisting of the fibers into a single thread of yarn. The direction of the twist may be clockwise (known as an S twist) or counterclockwise (a Z twist). All yarn resulting from this initial twisting is known as a singles yarn. Loosely twisted yarns are soft-spun yarns, whereas tightly twisted yarns are called hard-spun. Singles will contain varying amounts of fiber and differing poundage. When two singles are plied by twisting them together, they form a two-ply yarn. Three singles twisted together form a three-ply yarn, and so on. Two singles formed by twisting clockwise in an S twist are plied by turning counter-

Flat-woven pillow of unspun wool. Collection Jan Silberstein

Plying yarn by twisting single strands together in one direction and the doubled strands together in the opposite direction

clockwise in a Z twist. Similarly, if the original twist was a Z twist, the plying must be executed in an S twist. This reversing of the direction of the twists is the plying that keeps the group of strands interlocked.

Wool usually is sold by its textural description, fiber content, the number of singles plied together. In addition, a conscientious supplier will list the approximate yardage in each pound of yarn. The thickness of a particular yarn can often be visualized when you know the yardage in a pound. For instance, one pound of primitive woolen homespun yarn might contain about 500 yards as compared to 3500 yards in one pound of very fine weaving worsted. If there are very many yards to the pound, obviously the yarn must be a fine-spun one, provided the fiber content is the same. The difference between a wool yarn and a worsted yarn is in the carding and spinning. Worsted is processed more

Tapestry-woven wall hanging by Irja Mikkola

Peruvian rug. Collection of the author

Eighteenth-century French Aubusson chair covering. Collection of the author

Wall hanging by Saul Borisov. Collection Dr. and Mrs. H. Amsterdam

Wool and linen wall hanging by the author

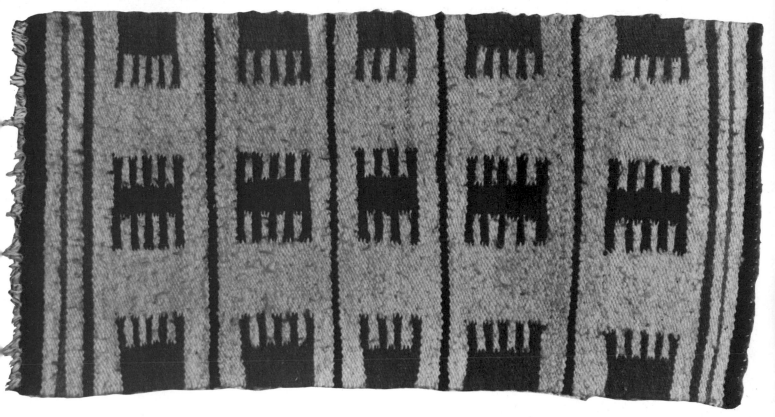

elaborately, requiring additional combing out and arranging of fibers for a smoother, softer thread. Worsted yarn is used in fine weaving and for knitting.

Buying yarn in small amounts is costly. Always check the number of ounces in small packets and divide the amount into the sixteen ounces that equal one pound. Multiply this figure by the cost of the packet to find the per-pound cost. Buying yarn by the pound from companies specializing in the product or from craft suppliers is always less expensive than buying it in a small retail shop. The best way to order yarn from a supplier is to request samples, inquiring at the same time about the yardage.

Plied yarns of different weights and thicknesses, usually cotton and linen, are designated by two numbers. The numbering system was designed by manufacturers to determine the yardage in a pound of yarn. They assign a third grading number to each type of fiber, based on its weight. It could be fine, medium, or heavy. For the manufacturer the higher number means a finer thread. A number 1 linen of a certain type has approximately 300 yards per pound. A number 2 linen would be figured at 2 times 300 yards and therefore would contain 600 yards per pound. For instance, a linen rug warp might be described in the supplier's catalogue listing as 8/5. The first number indicates the number of singles of a certain weight used to make a strand, and the second number indicates the number of strands twisted together. If a number 1 linen containing 300 yards per pound was used, the manufacturer would arrive at the yardage in this manner:

$$8 \div 5 = 1.60 \times 300 = 580 \text{ yards per pound}$$

There are many variables in this factor, and even the most reliable suppliers' catalogues are not fully detailed. All given amounts are approximations. Novelty twists and combination blends are difficult to calculate, and where there is uncertainty it is best to request the yardage from the manufacturer. Reliable sources and experience provide the best references. Extravagant overbuying is wasteful, and yet it is always sensible to have more than enough

Author weaving on a frame loom in South Brent, England. Photo John Evenden

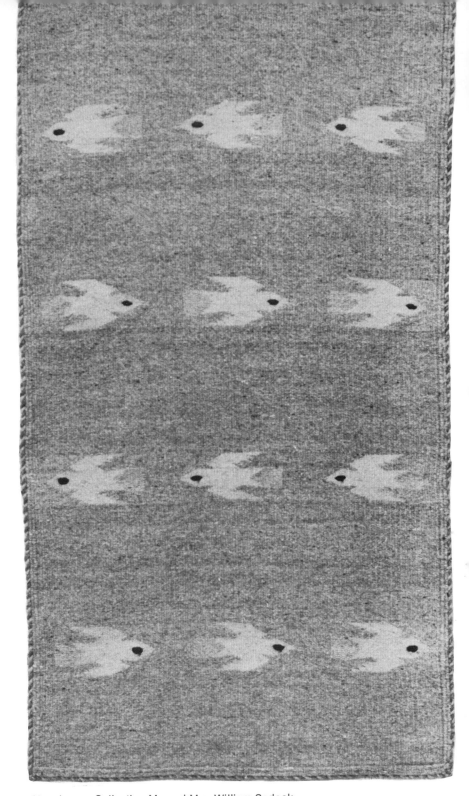

Navajo rug. Collection Mr. and Mrs. William Sadock

rather than too little on hand. Large craft suppliers whose basic business is dealing with public schools and other mass buyers will have a standardized product that can be ordered and reordered at a later date. Close-outs or special buys should be bought in sufficient quantity to make the complete piece. Leftover yarn can always be utilized, but yarns purchased separately may not be from the same dye lot and therefore may differ slightly in color. Unsuitable colors that are light in value can be dyed to blend with other colors. Rarely can they be dyed to match other colors. Darker colors are easily dyed black, a serviceable staple for most weavers.

Tapestry after Robert Motherwell's "Elegy to the Spanish Republic." Courtesy Pace Editions, Inc.

GLOSSARY

WARP
Spaced parallel threads running vertically.

WEFT
Horizontal filling threads woven over and under the spaced warp threads.

CUT HEDDLES

An arrangement of short cords encircling every other warp thread as an aid in separating and pulling the warp threads forward.

CONTINUOUS HEDDLES

An uncut, looped arrangement of cord encircling alternate warp threads across the entire weaving width.

HEDDLE BAR

A dowel or round rod holding the continuous heddles and a device for grasping and pulling all alternate threads forward at once.

SHED

An open space provided for the weft thread by raising the alternate warp threads with the heddles.

SHED STICKS
Flat narrow sticks designed to help maintain the separation and regularity of the warp threads.

BATTEN OR SWORD STICK
A flat, smoothly finished, bevel-edged stick with rounded ends for insertion in the open shed. The batten placed on end will hold the shed open and free both hands.

SHUTTLE
A tool for holding and carrying the weft thread across the shed.

BUBBLING

A method of loosely placing the weft in the shed in a series of small arcs.

BEATER
A tool with widely spaced tines for packing the weft down tightly.

SELVAGE

Edges of a fabric strengthened to prevent raveling.

TAPESTRY WEAVE

The most common weave. The weft is beaten down so closely as to cover the warp completely.

39

Weaving on a slack warp would be as unsuccessful as playing the guitar on loose strings or attempting to slam a ball across a net to the back court with a tennis racket strung in a relaxed manner. Tension was produced in the looms of ancient Greece by the weight of the rocks in the tied-together warp strings. A backstrap loom is tensioned by the thrust of the weaver's body. The warp is tied to a rod, and with the help of straps the rod is tied around the hips of the weaver. When the bar at the opposite end is attached to a tree, the weaver can tighten or release the tension at will by leaning backward or forward.

FRAME LOOMS FOR TAPESTRY RUGS AND WALL HANGINGS

A basic frame for weaving a rug or wall hanging can be constructed in the same manner as the one for twining. The significant difference is in the addition of an arrangement for opening a shed. Since pre-Grecian times the heddle and its holding rod have been used to pull the alternate threads forward, opening a space, called the shed, for the passage of the weft filling. The concept of looping cords around the warp threads to pull them open is so sensible and simple that there has been little if any change in their design.

Small experimental work can be woven on an artist's canvas stretcher. Even a small sturdy picture frame is suitable, particularly for classroom students in the early grades. Be aware, however, that the workable area of a frame loom measuring 16" × 20" is small. At best a finished piece will mea-

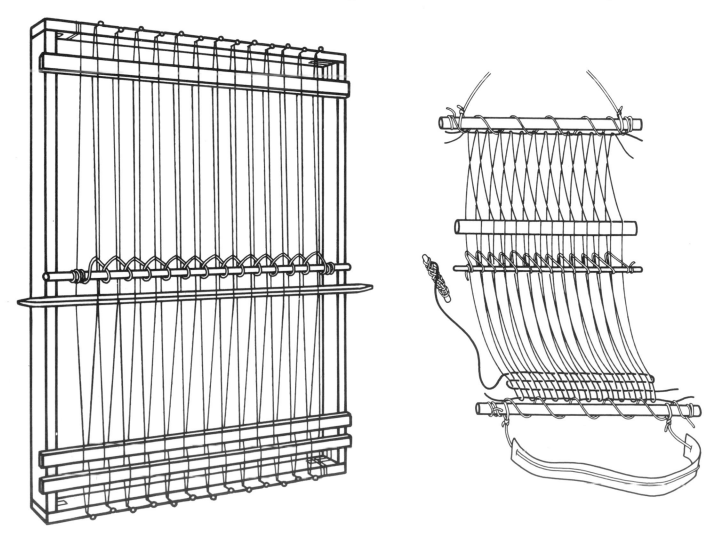

Frame loom

Backstrap loom

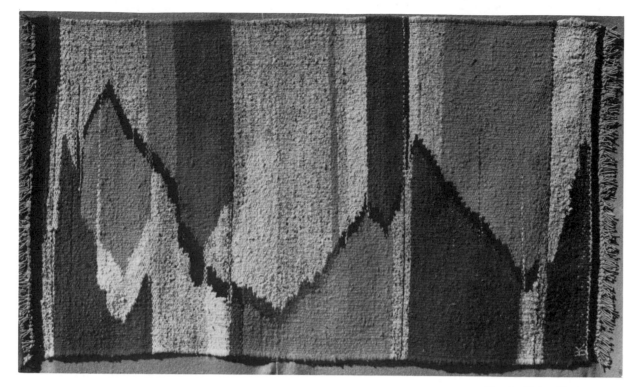

sure only 9″ × 11″, sufficient for a pillow top or a modest wall hanging. Sections of a design can be worked individually and assembled upon completion into a larger piece. Because the thin, inexpensive wood used in stretcher strips has a tendency to warp under tension in sizes over 28″ or 30″, do not depend upon them for larger frames. Larger sizes should be constructed of lumber at least 1″ thick and 2″ wide. The frame loom is usually thought of as a portable lap loom. Sizes larger than the arm can reach, in any direction, are impractical. Larger frame looms should be self-supporting in some manner, as is the Navajo loom; otherwise consider using an upright or horizontal tapestry and rug loom.

Additional equipment for the tapestry frame are three shed sticks and a sword stick. The sword stick is sometimes referred to as a batten. The shed sticks and the sword stick are cut from 3/16″ × 1 1/8″ lath. It is important that these sticks be long enough to overlap the side bars of the frame loom. Smooth and round both ends of the sword stick, tapering the 3/16″ thickness of the ends with sandpaper. Utilize all small pieces of lath for shuttles to carry the yarn across the warp. Of course, flat shuttles can be purchased, but they are easily made from lath stripping. Cut and file a rounded opening on both ends. Sand the entire shuttle to a smooth finish. It is handy to have in readiness at least three shuttles, particularly when several colors are used on a single piece. The most useful sizes are 8″, 12″, and 18″. Yarn for narrow sections can be wound into butterflies. Use 1/2″ doweling for a heddle rod spanning a 2′ width, and 3/4″ doweling for a 3′ width.

WARPING THE FRAME

Although the frame can be warped for tapestry in the same manner as for twining, less warp thread is used and the workable area can be made somewhat larger on a frame loom of heavy construction if the warp is wrapped around nails evenly spaced across the top and bottom of the frame. Use nails that have heads and are 1″ or more in length. Rule a center line along the length of the top and bottom bars of the frame. Space the nails 1/8″, 3/16″, or 1/4″ apart. Narrow spacing is correct for thinner yarn and will produce tight, firm

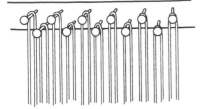

Warping over nails

work. Nails spaced 1/8″ apart permit the use of 1/4″ spacing on the same frame, by skipping every other turn around the nails. Mark the spaced measurements on the ruled line, starting 3″ in from the side of the frame and stopping 3″ from the opposite end. This 3″ space on either side of the warp is necessary to make room for handling the shuttle. Hammer the nails in halfway or more if they are more than 1″ long. They must not be loose. The nails should protrude about 1/2″.

A frame warped in this manner produces a single working surface between the nails on the upper and lower bars. Another method of warping is to provide tracks across the top and bottom, enabling the warp to be wound continuously around both the front and back of the frame. As these tracks cannot be spaced as closely as nails, in order to have six or eight warp threads to the inch it is necessary to place two or three threads in each track and space them after warping with twining or chaining. To bring the warp on around the frame and make the weaving continuous, the twining, shed sticks, and heddles may have to be removed. Because of the weft take-up, an allowance for additional warp and tensioning must be considered. Warping only the front of the frame loom is recommended. It is simple to assemble sections into larger pieces.

Usually the warp on tapestry-woven rugs and wall hangings is fully covered. Choose a strong fiber in a neutral color. An 8/5 linen or another very close weight combination, such as 8/4 or 10/5, is the most durable material for a large, heavy rug and is also the least likely to break while work is in progress. A strong cotton warp or a fiber mixture might be a second choice. Another prerequisite for warp thread is that it should not be stretchy. This point is important when choosing a warp that is to be exposed as a design element in a wall hanging. Any thread that breaks easily under tension is unsuitable. Most yarns will break when pulled between your hands, and are intended for weft filling, not warping.

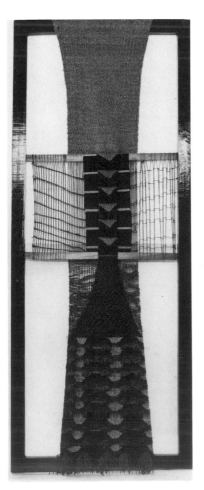

Tapestry panel by Anne Hunter

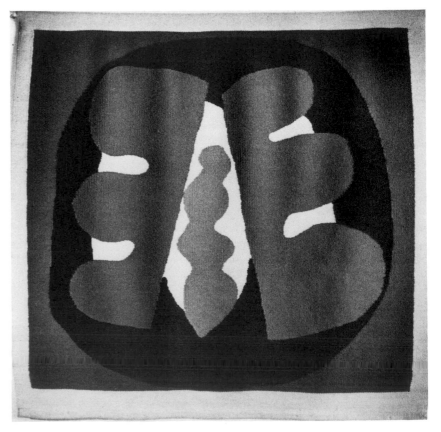

Yellow Heart and Tie by Irja Mikkola. Tapestry-woven wall hanging

Pell Del Poble by Josep Grau-Garriga. Courtesy Arras Gallery

WARP CALCULATION

Each vertical length of warp placed on a loom can be counted. These lengths are referred to for counting purposes as warp ends. The number of warp ends in an inch is called the sett. To determine the number of warp ends needed it is necessary to decide in advance on the width of the piece. The number of warp ends per inch—the sett—multiplied by the width equals the total number of warp ends. Therefore a sett of 8 ends to 1″ multiplied by a width of 12″ equals 96 warp ends. Find the amount of warp yardage needed by multiplying the number of warp ends by the length of the weaving area. An additional amount of warp must be added to allow room for the weft filling, which takes up a certain amount of room when it is inserted between the sheds. For a frame loom, allow at least two or three extra lengths. Make no attempt to figure out a precise amount of warping thread for a frame loom, except to be certain there will be enough warp on hand to complete the process once it has been started. Never knot the warp on the working surface. If nails are used to hold the warp, any joining of cut ends necessary should occur above or below the nails at the top and bottom of the frame. Warp the loom on a flat surface; one of table height is preferable. Start the warping at the bottom right-hand side of the frame by tying the warp around the bar several times. Bring the warp up and around the first nail at the top of the loom, down and around the one opposite it on the bottom bar. Continue until the opposite side is reached. Sometimes, after the warp has been tied on the bottom bar, turning the loom sideways and warping from left to right is more comfortable. Finish the process by tying the warp around the top bar at the opposite side. Do not pull the warp tight. The warp must be gently soft upon completion, not sagging but with a little slack, to allow for the easy insertion of the shed sticks. The purpose of two of the shed sticks is to take up this slack until the weft filling begins to tighten the warp. The shed sticks are then removed one at a time to lessen the tension. If the warp does become too tight during warping, smartly pat and press the flat of the hand against the center to loosen it, before final tying at the top.

INSERTING THE SHED STICKS

Insert the first shed stick at the bottom of the loom, working it over and under, over and under every thread. Start the second shed stick right above the first one, threading it through the warp in the reverse order, under and over, under and over, all across the row. Work carefully and with accuracy, checking the cross between the two sticks for regularity. If a thread is missed, withdraw the stick and start again. Both shed sticks will rest on the sides of the frame. Raise the second shed stick to open the warp and place the third stick just above it in the same shed. Move the third stick up to the top of the frame loom. The function of the two sticks at the bottom of the frame is to tighten the tension, and they remain stationary. The shed stick at the top of the loom moves up and down as needed to open one of the sheds.

HEDDLES

Cut the heddle rod long enough to overlap the side bars of the frame. A rod the correct length will rest on top of the loom frame. The heddles should be made of sturdy, inexpensive white cotton cord. Butcher cord is a good choice. The continuous heddle is an ingenious Navajo method of looping a cord around all the alternate warp threads so that the entire second shed can be opened by a single pull on the heddle rod. It works well in lengths under 36″. Each heddle will require about 5″ of cord to be used on every other warp

Shed sticks inserted in warp

A Town Inside the Ramparts by Lea Tennberg

thread, or half the total number of warp ends. Allow an extra 10″ or 12″ for attaching the cord to the heddle rod. Knots in the heddle cord are annoying, so be sure to roll enough cord into a small ball to make an uninterrupted continuous heddle. Tie one end around the heddle rod several times and knot the end to affix it to the rod.

Place the heddle rod on the warp in the center of the frame, holding one end in the hand. Bring the upper shed stick down from the top until it is about 8″ away from the heddle rod. Push the ball of cord under the first warp thread emerging from under the shed stick. If threaded correctly this will be the second thread from the end. The heddles will lift the alternate threads (the ones not controlled and lifted by the shed stick). Draw the cord forward, over the heddle rod, around and through the opening to the right. Do not pull the cord up tightly. Skip the thread over the shed stick and pass the ball of thread under the next one, bringing it over the heddle rod and through the space to the right. Each heddle should be about 2½″ long. As the heddles are being made, lift the rod about 2½″ above the warp and slowly run the rod and heddles a short way up and down the warp to regulate the length of the heddles. In a continuous heddle the lengths of each heddle will automatically adjust to the height the rod is held above the warp.

Continue across the warp until each alternate thread is held by a heddle. Tie the end of the cord to the bar with a few half hitches. Move the upper shed

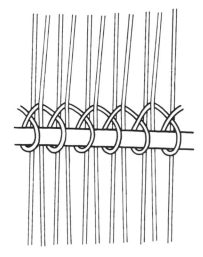

Continuous heddle

Dried flower container by Sharon Seelig. Photo Barry Seelig

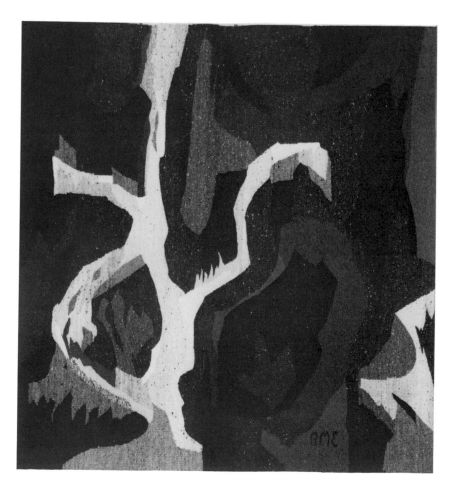

Dialogue by Rose-Marie Eggmann. Photo François Martin

Left and above: Front and back of a frame loom for tapestry. Courtesy Gunnel Teitel

Holding devices

stick back to the top of the loom. Lift the heddle rod and run it up and down the warp several times to check the length of each heddle. Place the sword stick through the shed provided when the heddle rod is lifted. Turn the stick on edge and the shed will remain open without holding the rod, freeing the hands. Change the shed by removing the sword stick, bringing the upper shed stick down into position, and turning it on edge to open the alternate shed. The upper shed stick is never removed; it remains in the warp until the weaving is completed. If the heddle rod does not lift up easily it is because the upper shed stick has not been moved up toward the top of the loom. This small frame loom is based on the same operating principle as any professional two-harness rug loom. The harness is the frame on a loom designed to hold the heddles through which the alternate warp is threaded.

Innovative changes and adaptations in details of the structure of the loom are made by all weavers as their experience increases. There are many inexpensive home devices that offer possibilities for securing the heddle rod and holding the warp. The hardware store is a source for a variety of small items for holding round rods, such as equipment for hanging curtains and drapes, large cup hooks, screw eyes, and the much-used C-clamp. Weavers often attach a C-clamp to the edge of the frame, and by raising the heddle rod onto the long end of the clamp, manage to hold the shed open without inserting the sword stick. The famous Gobelin tapestry loom is designed with a fixed heddle rod, similar to the hollow steel bars used to construct a child's jungle gym. Very long continuous heddles are attached to the bar. Each heddle is evenly spaced and held in position by half hitches that eliminate movement and maintain the fixed length of the heddles. The shed is opened by hand-pulling on groups of heddles in selected sections. The purpose of this type of heddling is that it holds them conveniently up and away from the working area. As many weavers seated next to each other work on a single piece at one time, this method

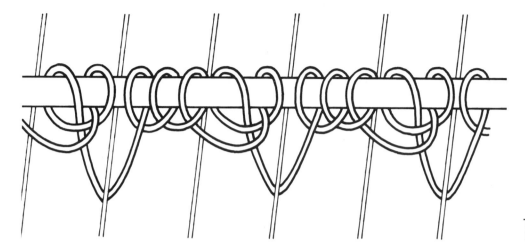

allows the individual weaver to open a shed as needed at almost any stage as the work progresses. Lengths of cord encircling alternate warp threads without a heddle rod would work almost as well on a modest-size tapestry.

Winding the warp all around the frame loom to weave an additional length of fabric without rewarping requires a strong warp and an extra length of warp for the take-up as the filling expands the sheds. Prepare the frame in advance for the necessary excess by taping a 3″ width of tightly folded newspaper, about ⅜″ thick (or the equivalent in cardboard), along the top and bottom of both the front and back of the loom. Of course, more or less might be needed, depending upon the thickness of the weft selected. Remove the newspaper in gradual stages as the increasing tightness of the tension makes it difficult to turn the shed or sword stick on end.

THE NAVAJO LOOM

An adaptation of the Navajo Indian loom is practical for releasing the tension on rugs. However, it requires separate warping on a temporary frame, a preliminary step before attaching the warp to the loom. Navajo rugs have four selvages because of this separate warping. Determine the finished length of the piece to be woven and space two 1″ dowels this distance apart. The Navajos use two selected slender tree trunks, stripped and prepared, lashing them at right angles on top of two other thick, heavier ones placed on the ground, thus automatically raising the warping poles off the ground and providing a space for the hands and the ball of warping material. The Indian weaver sits on the ground in the center of this open rectangle, warping from left to right in a figure eight. Warping on the floor or ground may be comfortable; if it is, use two-by-fours raised above the working surface with cinder blocks at each corner, or support the two-by-fours on two chair seats placed facing each other. Arrange the two-by-fours any distance apart greater than the width of the piece to be woven. If there is room, place the two-by-fours sufficiently far apart so there is space to stand within the frame. Hammer nails in each piece of lumber, at a point about 2″ shorter than the finished length of the weaving. Allow the heads of the nails to protrude about 1″. Place the dowels outside the nails, lashing them to the two-by-fours with strong twine. Determine the desired width of the woven piece. Within this measurement, pencil short guidelines ¼″ apart on both dowels. Tie the warping yarn around one of the dowels by bringing the cut end 4″ down from under the dowel and tying the end of the warp to itself in a square knot. Bring the warp over the opposite dowel, around and under; continue back to the other side. Always place the warp over the dowels and return the warp under the dowels in a figure eight. Space each turn ¼″ apart, following the penciled guidelines. End the warp on the same dowel on which it started, tying it again with a square knot about 4″ from the dowel.

Carrying the warp over the dowels is called a warp turn, and each turn makes a pair of warp threads. The cross in the warp created by the figure eight establishes the two sheds necessary for tapestry weaving. A shed stick placed in each side of the figure eight preserves the shed. Tie the two shed sticks together at both ends after drawing them close together at the center of the warp. Indian weavers use long, slender branches, usually from birch

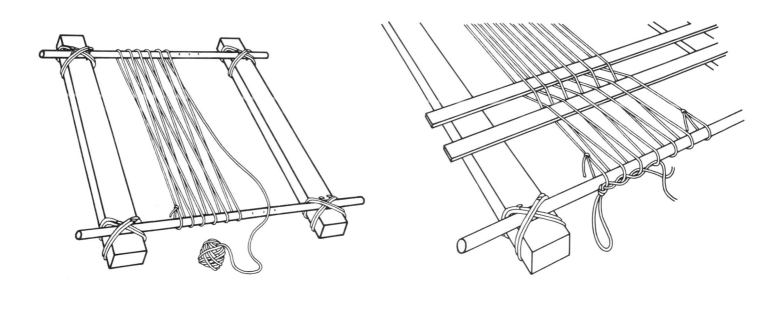

Warping for the Navajo loom. Above: Winding the warp on the dowels. Above, right: Twining the warp ends with the shed sticks inserted. Right: Binding the twined edges to the dowels

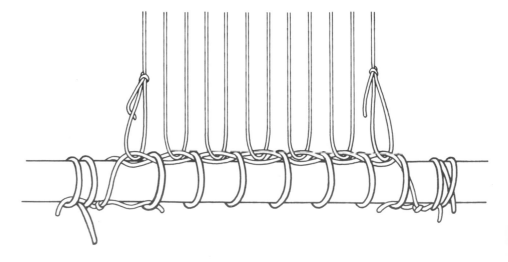

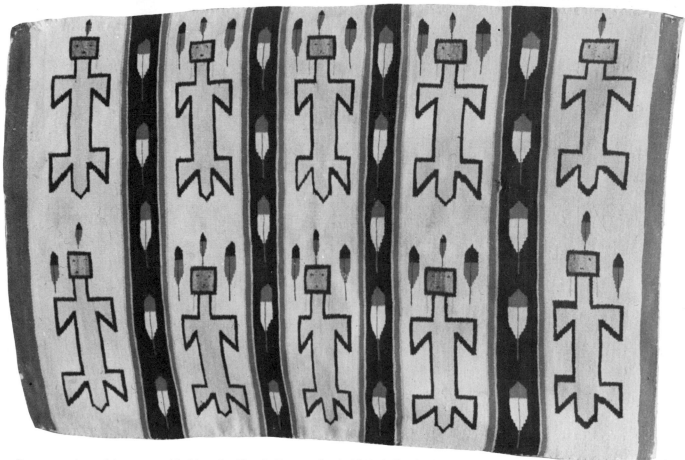

Rug woven by a sixteen-year-old girl on the Navajo Reservation in 1949. Collection Dr. and Mrs. Theodore R. Sadock

trees, as shed sticks. After peeling off the bark and any small branches, they soak the stick and tie it to a straight stake until it is completely dry and straightened. One of these round sticks is used as the heddle rod; the other remains in place. Contemporary weavers could use a lath shed stick and a slender dowel, or two flat shed sticks, replacing one later on with a heddle rod.

Prepare a weft for twining by doubling over a length of two-ply rug yarn of a length suitable for the width of the piece. As this row of weft twining will become an integral part of the weaving, it should match the colors selected for the top and bottom of the design. Tie an overhand knot 5″ from the folded end. The twining starts right at the end of the warp turn, and is worked down until it is positioned just inside the dowel. Measure and maintain the desired width of the weaving. As each turn was spaced ¼″ apart and the turn is the equivalent of 2 warp ends, the measure is 8 warp ends per inch. A 24″ width would contain 192 warp ends. Repeat the twining on the opposite dowel. Be certain each warp turn is included in the twining. If the measurements of both sides do not agree, slide the warp turns closer together or farther apart and gently pull up the weft. Tie the twining ends together at the end of each row. Allow at least 5″ of extra yarn to extend beyond the tied end. Cut off the excess yarn.

BINDING THE WARP

Proceeding very slowly, taking great care not to disturb the twined edges, lift the dowels and the warp from the temporary frame. Place the warp on the floor, laying it out flat, as straight and as smooth as it was on the frame. Slowly remove the dowels, but do not remove the shed sticks. Using the same dowels, center each one outside the warp edging. Cut the end of the 5″ loop at the beginning of the weft twining on the left side. Tie the cut ends to the dowel

Wall hanging by Michael Cornfeld

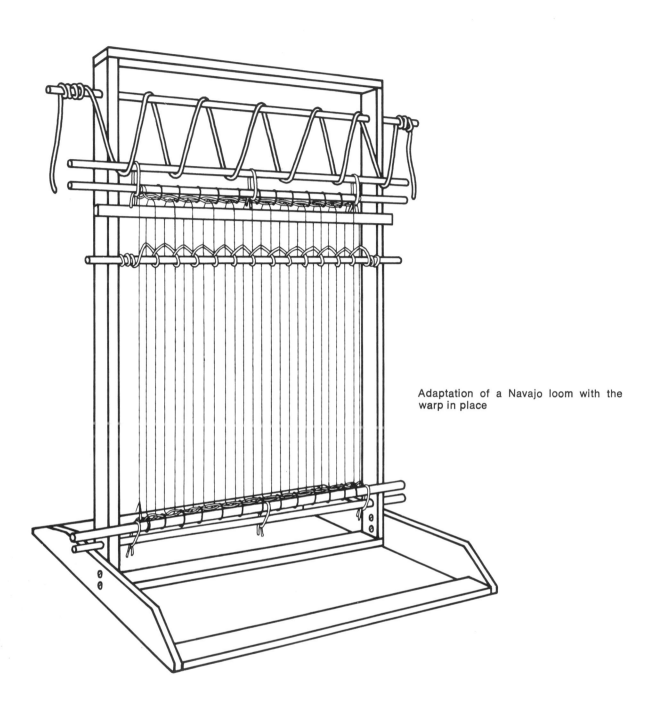

Adaptation of a Navajo loom with the warp in place

tightly, just a bit to the left of the warp. Tie the other end tightly to the right of the warp. Repeat this on the second dowel, centering it on the opposite side. Use very strong cord to bind the warp to the dowel. If there is any doubt about the strength of the cord, double it because weaving increases the warp tension and the binding is the crucial point of attachment to the loom frame. Prepare a sufficient length of cord in advance. Attach the cord to the dowel, wrapping it around and over the tied weft end. Tightly bind the warp to the dowel by passing the cord over the twining through the spaces between the warp turns. It may be helpful to prepare a long cord by winding it onto a flat shuttle. Use the 1/4" pencil marks as a guide. After completing the binding, secure the end of the cord to the dowel. Repeat on the opposite side.

MOUNTING THE WARP

Never weave on a crooked warp. The warp must always be perpendicular to a horizontal plane—in other words at right angles to the bars. With the warp still on the floor, tie the upper dowel to a third dowel in three places if it is of modest length, and in five places on longer ones. Prepare six or more 15" pieces of picture wire or very strong twine, half for the top bar and the other half for the bottom. The upper warping dowel and the third dowel must be tied a uniform distance from each other with the wire or strong twine. Maintain this uniformity by placing a temporary gauge between the bars. The perfect distance between the two bars is about 1". Use a piece of lath or a dowel as a gauge. Place ties on either side of the warp, centering others equidistant from the side ties. Work the ones in the center of the warp beneath and around the twined edging cord.

After centering the warp between the posts of the self-supporting loom, tie the bottom dowel containing the warp to the pole inserted in the lower section of the frame, tying it as tightly as possible. The upper and lower poles in the frame loom correspond to beams and are called beams by manufacturers of large looms. They must be able to resist sagging under tension. Consider using a metal pipe or solid metal curtain rod for your beam. A rope or length of heavy braided clothesline is necessary for suspending the upper dowel containing the warp from the upper beam. Attach one end of the rope to the end of the upper beam where it extends outside the frame. Carry the rope under the third dowel, up and over the top beam, down and under the dowel, up and over

Rockface by Robert Mabon. Tapestry and plain weave with some Soumak, woven on simple frame loom

Petita Gestacio by Josep Grau-Garriga. Courtesy Arras Gallery

the beam. Tie the rope to the extension of the upper beam at the opposite end. At all times the warp must be held under tension to avoid ripples on the side edges and in the fabric of the weaving. Any adjustments take place in the rope between the third dowel and the upper beam. Pull up on the rope in front with one hand, down on the rope behind the beam with the other hand. Transfer hands with each set of the rope without releasing the tension for a moment until the warp is taut and even across the entire width. Retie the rope when you reach the other end. Most likely the warp will need tightening every so often at the beginning, or until the weft filling expands the warp. It is a good idea to loosen the tension when work is stopped for prolonged periods.

OPENING THE SHED

Untie the shed sticks, pushing the top one upward. The stick is positioned under alternate threads in readiness for opening a shed by turning the stick on edge. If two flat lath sticks have been used, turn the lower one on end to open the second shed. Select a heddle rod, a ½″ or ⅝″ dowel, depending upon the warp width. Place it against the raised warp threads and attach a continuous Navajo heddle, using medium-weight cord.

After the heddles are attached to every other thread raised by the shed stick, remove the stick. You will then be able to open this shed by pulling the heddle rod forward and inserting a separate sword stick or batten to hold the shed open.

Maintaining a strong, straight selvage is a primary consideration. The Navajos control the spacing initially with the edging cord, then stabilize the warp with tight binding, and finally by regulating the warp tension. If the warp is tight and the spacing correct, it is unlikely that the form will become distorted while the weaving is in progress. Some weavers strengthen the edges by arranging the heddles and shed stick so that two warp threads on either edge function as one. Some Indian weaving shows a supplementary pair of warp cords alternately incorporated in the weft turns on either side. This method affects the aesthetics of the piece, particularly if the cord is of a contrasting color. Another special element of most Navajo weaving occurs in the first and last rows. The weft is woven under and over every pair of warp turns by hand before the shedding device, designed to open every other thread, is brought into play.

A backstrap loom is warped in exactly the same manner as described for the Navajo loom except for mounting the warp on a self-supporting frame. After the warping has been removed from the temporary warping frame, a holding cord is attached to the top bar and the backstrap to the lower bar. Only five sticks are used to construct the entire backstrap loom.

TAPESTRY WEAVING

Rugs and wall hangings are often woven with an inch of plain weave at both ends, matching weft color to the warp. This inch of plain weave stabilizes the warp on the loom, provides a horizontal base for weaving, and in the case of rugs protects the edges from excessive wear. If desired, these sturdy ends can be folded under and hemmed. Hemming may be desirable on a wall hanging, but it limits the reversible potential of a tapestry-woven rug. Sometimes crushed tissue paper or very thick yarn is woven in for an inch or two at the beginning to stabilize warp, and is removed when the piece has been completed. All weaving starts at the bottom, or the beam nearest to the seated weaver, and proceeds upward. Prepare the yarn in advance on long flat

Flat-weave tube by Peter Collingwood

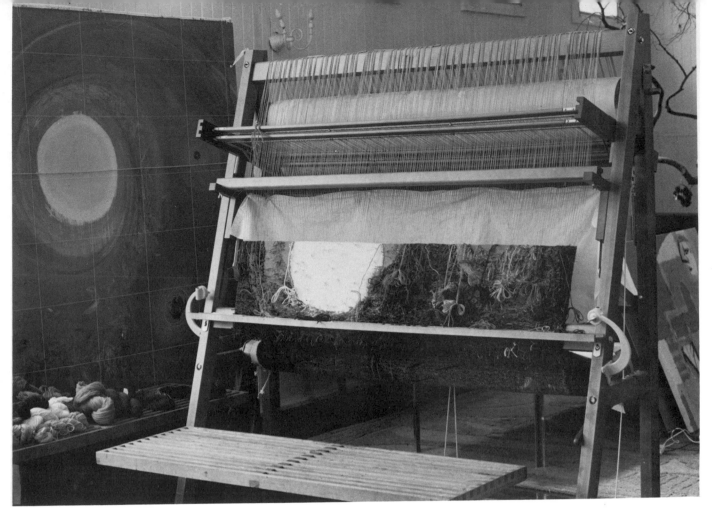

Weaving in progress on a frame loom. Photo Edmund Marein

Partly completed tapestry woven by Sally Shore. Courtesy Mr. and Mrs. Erwine Laverne

shuttles for large areas of solid color and smaller shuttles, butterflies, and bobbins for smaller areas. Do not overwind bobbins and butterflies. Bulky masses become difficult to push through the sheds, and they loosen and tangle before large amounts are utilized. Untangling knots and rewinding yarn slows the pace.

In Europe five centuries of tapestry weavers brought the basic technique of mural painting with yarn to the peak of perfection during the seventeenth and eighteenth centuries. Weavers spent almost eight years learning and practicing the precise and absolute discipline of transcribing the work of recognized artists. Skilled weavers concentrated on the mechanical processes, totally uninvolved with the creative or visual aspects of the work. Just as the typographer sets type upside down and backwards, the traditional tapestry weaver, at Aubusson for instance, still works on a horizontal loom with the front of the tapestry facing down. The working surface facing the weaver is obscured by short ends, loose threads, and hanging bobbins. During the eighteenth century as many as two thousand colors were sometimes used in a single piece to express intricately shaded figures and foliage. Hundreds of hanging snippets of yarn were unwound from small flutelike bobbins. Today's artist-craftsman faces the front surface of the work, deals directly with color and texture, creates directly on the loom from an idea, or if a sketch is used, freely interprets the design according to his own emotional or intellectual dictates.

Today we are free to sketch directly on the warp strings with Magic Markers.

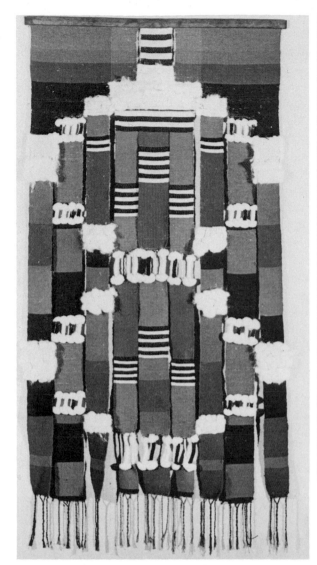

Slit Tapestry by Melissa Cornfeld

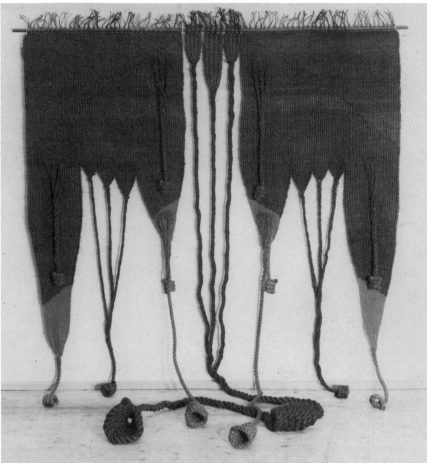

He-Tapestry by David Holbourne

Sometimes it is a good idea to mark the halfway point when the entire warp is stretched on a frame loom. Even further divisions are helpful, particularly if a sketch is used as a guide. Open a shed to divide the warp threads and insert the shuttle carrying the weft. Drop the cut end of the weft between two warp strands near the center. (Never start or finish weft yarn at the edges.) Always stop at least four warp ends from the selvage. No cut ends should ever appear at the selvages. The selvages are always finished with weft turns. Keep the shed open while positioning the weft. Push the shuttle through in an upward diagonal, then arrange the weft by holding it in position with one hand while placing the opposite side at least 6″ above horizontal. This diagonal slant supplies the extra weft necessary for the take-up that occurs when the alternate shed is opened. As slender as the warp may seem, each shot or pick of weft across it goes under and over, under and over, using up more weft than is at first apparent. Push the weft down with the index finger in a series of scallops or bubbles to insure an even distribution of extra weft across the width of the rug warp. Close the shed and beat the weft down with a beater. A professional beater is composed of a thick, short wooden handle with evenly spaced steel tines that easily fall between each warp thread. Handmade beaters with wooden tines are made from a single piece of wood with the handle carved to fit the curves of the hand. However, a fork or comb with widely spaced teeth will work adequately. Tapestry requires firm beating in order to cover the weft fully.

Sacking needle

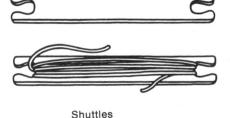

Shuttles

55

TWO-COLOR STRIPE OR SLIT

Insert the yarn through the open shed from the left or right, stopping at the point where you wish to make the color change, and bring the shuttle forward. Using another shuttle containing the change of color, drop about 4″ of the cut end between the warp ends where the last shuttle emerged, and continue to the other side with the new color. Close the shed and beat the weft down. When two colors are used vertically, the shuttles can approach each other from the left and the right. Change the shed and pass the shuttles back again; continue back and forth, changing the shed at each turn. This method of placing two colors next to each other vertically with weft turns between them produces the open slit common to all kilim rugs and tapestries. The slits are invisibly sewn together on the reverse side of some tapestry wall hangings. There is a practical limit to the length of the slit openings on rugs. About 1″ is sensible, adding a decorative flicker and some dimension to the quality of the flat-woven rug. The vertical stripe may be continued upward by interlocking or linking the two wefts together at the meeting point, before the shuttle is turned back.

Another method of holding the warp slit together is by dovetailing. In dovetailing, the weft turn of the two colors is made on the same warp end, alternating one color above the other. The weaving progresses faster if the pick of weft goes back and forth two or three times before the adjacent color starts its turns around the same warp. Dovetailing is suitable only for vertical lines that are relatively short because of the heavy build-up of the two yarns on the single warp end.

DIAGONAL LINES

Diagonal lines can be made to go upward at a desired slant. The most pronounced slant is achieved by having one color advance two warp threads before the weft turn with regularity. An advance that progresses only one warp thread before the weft turn produces a lesser slant. The gentlest slant is worked with a vertical rise for two or three weft turns before it is advanced to the next warp thread.

OVALS AND CIRCLES

Ovals and circles are achieved through a calculated combination of vertical

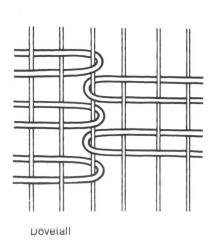

Slit

Dovetail

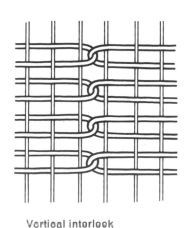

Vertical interlook

Detail of tapestry woven by Rosalie Adolf

56

rises and diagonal advances until the contour is completed. Better results can be obtained with ovals and circles if they are drawn first, cut out of paper, and traced onto the warp ends. Draw half of the rounded form on tracing paper, fold the tracing paper in half, and trace the other half. When the paper is opened out the form will be completely symmetrical. For a true circle use a compass or a large plate as a guide.

WEAVING PROBLEMS

Problems that occur in tapestry weaving often are related to each other and have a common cause. Controlling the selvage is one of the most usual. Pulling the weft too tightly will cause the edges to curve in like an hourglass.

Without being aware of the cause, you may suddenly realize that the warp ends have become grouped too closely together in one section. This problem becomes noticeable when the weft refuses to pack down after beating, having no room to go around each warp.

Another evidence of trouble ahead occurs when a high spot appears in a horizontal row. With insufficient room between close warp ends the weft will rise in spots and settle in others. Several factors can contribute to this problem.

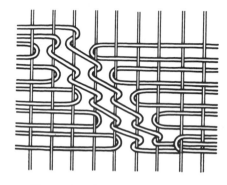

Diagonal outline

1. The warp may be loose and need tightening.
2. The weft may be laid too tightly in the shed.
3. The warp may be spaced too close together. In order to pack the weft down, fully covering the warp, fewer warp ends to the inch may be required. Eight ends to the inch is usually satisfactory for most weaving, but a thick weft filling often may be woven more efficiently on a warp spaced only six warp ends to the inch.

Keep a tape measure handy at all times. Determine by measurement when the width begins to change, and make corrections by taking out a few rows and adjusting your technique. Remember that when the weaving is plain or only a small pattern of simple horizontal stripes is introduced, there are few problems. Tightness more often occurs in complex patterns that require many linked or interlocked color changes.

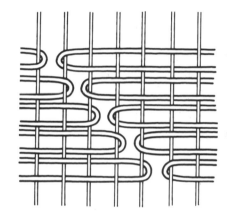

Diagonal slit

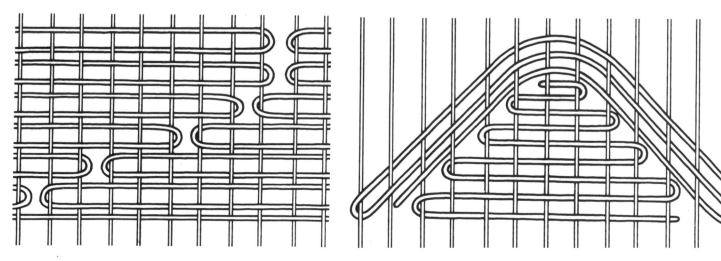

Rising curve

Curve

57

Steps in chaining

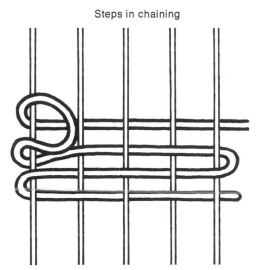

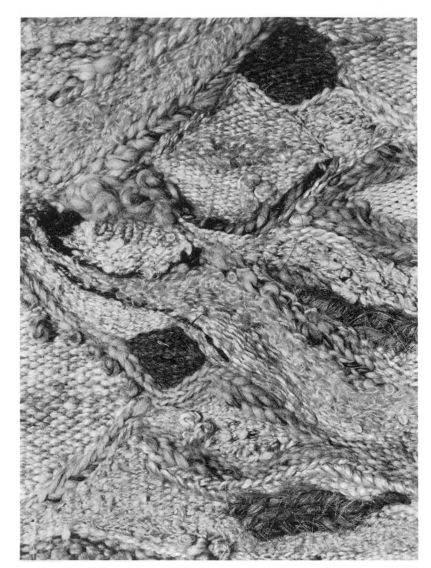

Curving tapestry-weave sample by Gunnel Teitel

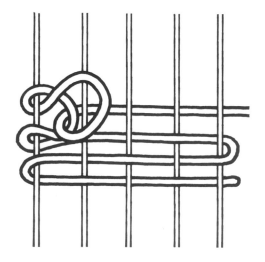

VARIATIONS

Chaining and Soumak, techniques borrowed from embroidery, are worked on a closed shed. Although an entire rug or wall hanging can be chained or worked in the Soumak stitch, the resulting fabric has a tendency to be flimsy. Because of the relative looseness of the stitches on the warp, the width stretches too much and individual rows move up and down on the warp too easily. Alternate rows of chaining or Soumak with plain tapestry weave.

CHAINING

This ageless embroidery stitch, in use for centuries by the Chinese as well as the Paracas Indians, has many facets. Weavers often use it to space the warp. It is a raised surface stitch, with little yarn used on the reverse side, and it produces the effect of a braid. Alternately spaced with inches of plain weave, chaining enhances textural quality when only one color is used throughout. Using a contrasting color for chaining produces horizontal stripes.

1. Start with a sturdy base of plain tapestry weave.
2. Free the weft from the shuttle, winding an excessive length into a butterfly.
3. Begin chaining on the left-hand side, with the weft emerging from underneath the end warp thread. If a contrasting color is used for the chaining, weave the cut end from the right to the left for about 3" before starting the chain.
4. Bring the weft out to the left. Form a modest-size loop large enough for your thumb and index finger. Bend it over the end warp toward the right. The free end of the weft will be under the loop.
5. Reach through the loop with the thumb and index finger, pulling up a new loop of weft yarn and bringing it over to the right. Tighten the first loop.
6. Continue across the warp threads, tightening the loops as the chaining progresses.
7. When the right selvage is reached, pass the end of the weft through the last loop, locking it in place. (Left unlocked, the entire row of chaining will pull out easily.) Use this end of the weft to continue with the succeeding rows of plain weave until the next row of chaining occurs in the desired pattern. If a contrasting color has been used, weave a few inches of this weft end back into the warp. The plain-weave weft color can then be picked up again and carried up to the next row. If the weft is of very thick yarn, incorporate the plain-weave weft with the end warp before the last chain takes place.

There is a tendency for the chained loops to turn over while being formed. A regular appearance depends upon maintaining untwisted chains. A very thick weft, such as jute, may spread the warp threads too far apart. Preserve the correct spacing by chaining over pairs of warp threads. A very thick chain will cover several rows of the plain weave on either side. Another variation in chaining will occur when two yarns of different colors are used in the plain-weave shed and then chained, alternating colors one row above the other.

SOUMAK

The design area can be raised above the flat-woven tapestry with the bold texture of the Soumak weave. Soumak, a name possibly derived from a Caucasian hamlet noted for the technique, was also practiced in many other weaving centers in the Middle East. Closely resembling a needlework stem stitch in both construction and appearance, Soumak is a process of wrapping weft around the warp threads on a closed shed. Soumak is sometimes woven without a flat-weave ground but is more practical when alternated with a few rows of plain weave. When fine yarn is used, as it is in Caucasian Soumak, the ground weaving is deceptively covered, giving the appearance of needlework embroidery. Soumak easily delineates small design areas in the center of flat weaves and can be thought of as laid-in brocading.

Using short butterflies, bring the weft over four warp threads, back under two threads, and forward again. Continue over four and under two, working across the warp. When the weft has been beaten down, short diagonal lines appear. If the weft is returned in the opposite direction, the diagonal lines will run counter to the row below.

There are many wrapping techniques, and the weaver can devise still others with additional combinations of twists and knots. Greek Soumak, or Greek knot, is another method of wrapping the warp. Work with a butterfly. Bring the yarn from behind the warp, holding the tail end out with the other hand. Wrap the yarn around the warp, under the tail end, and up and around the warp again. The warp can be wrapped three or more times before proceeding to the next warp.

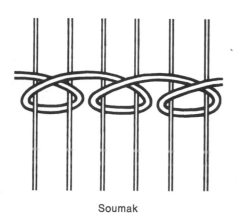

Soumak

Tapestry and Soumak with blended yarn colors

Greek Soumak

Tapestry and Soumak

60

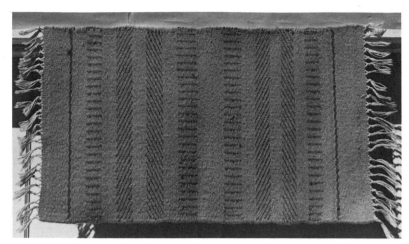
Rug by Edith Karlin

Tapestry with linen and leather

Two-color weave

WEAVING PATTERNS

A sturdy mat can be woven in no time at all on a frame loom using jute or sisal for both the warp and the weft. A 50/50 weave is one in which the weft is not packed down on the warp. The basket weave is woven with two wefts used together, or side by side, going over pairs of warp threads. Thinner jute can be worked with four weft threads over and under four warp threads. An equal amount of warp and weft is exposed. The mat will be fully reversible if each new piece of weft is laid in by overlapping several inches of the new weft over the one just finished. Very thick jute can be unplied at both ends, thinned a bit, and replied by twisting the two ends together. Jute twine requires wide warp spacing. Sheds are hardly necessary as the weft filling can be interlaced back and forth with the fingers.

COLOR WARPING

Exciting changes take place in a 50/50 weave when the warp colors are varied at intervals. Subtle color changes are achieved by keeping the range of colors close in value. Quiet low-key colors, such as grays, browns, and black, are subtle ones, harmonizing with each other, taking their place unobtrusively in their environment. Plaids and stripes in bright colors can also be subtle but provide a striking note of visual interest. A brightly colored warp can be toned back with a somber weft, then highlighted at intervals with a vividly colored weft.

VERTICAL STRIPES

Short rows of vertical bars are recommended for the impatient, if working on a close warp with two-ply yarn. Wind two shuttles with two contrasting colors. Weave one row with each color alternately. The weft must be firmly beaten down to show the bars clearly. Great care must be taken with the edges because the weft turns do not encircle the end warp. Without opening a shed, using two colors of heavy twine, you will find weaving speedier if the weft is woven over pairs of warp ends.

Tapestry with horizontal design in two colors

Series of V's. Wall hanging by Melissa Cornfeld

Wall hanging by Melissa Cornfeld. Collection
State of West Virginia. Photo by the author

Wall hanging by Tadek Beutlich. Tapestry weave with dyed sisal
Soumak weave. Courtesy Arras Gallery

LOOPED PILE

Both the Greeks and the Copts practiced a looping technique on flat-woven fabrics to produce a pile similar to that of Turkish toweling or terry cloth. In this method the uncut loops are formed from the weft threads. After the weft has been inserted in the shed, a pointed bamboo stick or slender branch is slid between the first and the second warp thread. The point is dipped under the weft, pulling it up in a loop. The loop is held on the stick as the point is slid over to pick up the weft again between the third and fourth warp thread, continuing in this manner all across the warp. All the loops are held on the stick while the shed is changed and a row of weft is inserted and beaten down to secure the loops. The stick is carefully removed and the weft and looped

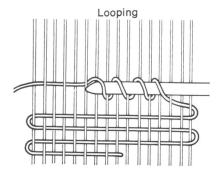

Looping

Wall hanging by Michael Cornfeld. Photo by the author

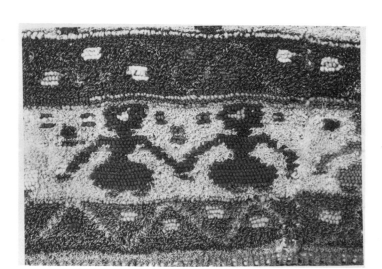

Above: Detail of looped pile with design of small figures, Crete. Collection Leon Pomerance. Below: Nineteenth-century looped pile, Crete. Detail. Collection Leon Pomerance

pile are firmly beaten down again. The looped fabric was developed for warmth and as a decorative relief from the flat weave. Velvet and corduroy are power-loom derivations of this technique.

Any number of rows of plain weave may be inserted between the rows of loops. Use a long knitting needle to pick up the loops, or sharpen the end of a long dowel in a pencil sharpener to make a longer pickup. Patterns can be arranged by skipping warp threads between loops as the design may indicate. Thicker loops are made by winding the shuttle with two wefts at the same time. Color changes may be introduced by winding supplementary yarn into a butterfly. A firm selvage should be maintained and the rows of plain weave beaten as tightly as possible to hold the loops in place.

Wall hanging by Melissa Cornfeld. Photo by the author

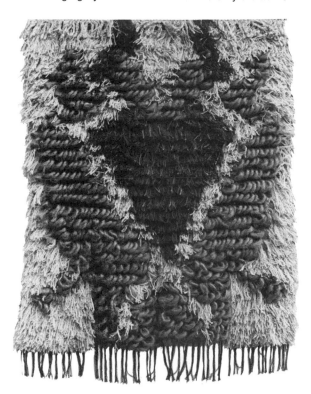

Tapestry weave with pickup loops

Hand-woven Portuguese rug with pickup loops. Collection Edith Karlin

WEFT-FACED RAG RUGS

Space a strong, slender cotton warp four ends to the inch. Prepare the rag weft in advance. Woolen, cotton, or jersey rags or surplus mill ends are all useful. It is not a good idea to mix rags of different fiber content. Aside from the problem of different rates of shrinkage, if all rags are cut the same width, some will be bulkier than others, causing high and low areas in the surface. Color is an important consideration when you are working with a miscellaneous assortment of odds and ends. Even a Hit-or-Miss pattern requires thoughtful choices, or one color will be concentrated in one place. A good random rug shows no sudden or congested pockets of color. A variation on the Hit-or-Miss scattered pattern can be arranged by separating the rags into piles of light, medium, and dark tonal values. Remember to come to a decision on color arrangement before cutting or tearing the rags into strips. Of course, the rags can be dyed in advance to any desired color.

Do not cut the strips on the bias. A rug should not stretch more than 1/2″ in width after the weft has been inserted. The width of the strips is a matter of choice that affects the appearance of the rug. Crush or fold a small cut piece in your hand as a sample. If scissors are used for cutting, measure distances

Flat-woven rug of rags by Gunnel Teitel

and rule lines on the cloth with a piece of chalk or a pencil as a guide to straight cutting. A cloth cutter can also be used. Seam short strips together, making lengths about 2½ times the width of the rug. Very long strips are difficult to maneuver through the sheds, becoming too bulky when wound on the shuttles. Long shuttles will hold more than short shuttles. As there will probably be no need for color changes related to a planned design, one long, flat shuttle will suffice. The strips can be wound on the shuttles without folding and crushed down with the beating. On the other hand, a neater, more formal treatment of the strips is to fold the cut edges in toward the center, then fold the strip in half again, burying the raw edges. Lay in all new strips by overlapping the cut ends about 2″ or 3″. Do not overbeat folded strips. Many fabrics and fibers can be woven. Some materials are suited only to wall hangings; others, somewhat fragile but decorative, can be woven into small hearth rugs or placed in positions (at the side of a bed, for instance) where they receive gentle wear. There are materials that are rather durable but not particularly suited to large rugs. Scrap leather is such a fabric. Scrap leather, like scrap vinyl, is best laid in the warp with no attempts at turning around the warp ends. Commercially, such rugs are often machine-stitched along the selvages.

THE FUR RUG

Many people save old fur coats, worn sheepskin jackets, or fur-type zip-out linings of the kind often found in children's outgrown snow suits. These scraps make fascinating rugs—sometimes genuine conversation pieces. Open all the seams carefully, cutting the stitches with a razor blade. Place all the pieces on a newspaper laid out on a table, pile side down. No folding is necessary; the strips should be cut to weaving size. About ⅜″ to ½″ is adequate. Use a ruler and felt-tip marker to measure and mark the strips accurately, with no waste. Cut along each ruled line on the hide with a very sharp razor blade or an X-acto knife. Cut and use every piece, no matter how big or small. Pieces as short as 2″ or 3″ can be utilized. The fur scraps must be supported in the warp with a rag base. Prepare long strips of soft rag 1″ wide. Old sheets or inexpensive muslin will do if no other suitable rags are available. Space a thin but strong cotton or natural-colored linen warp, four ends to the inch. Match the warp to the fur. Prepare to open the sheds with shed sticks and heddle rod. Weave two rows of rag to stabilize the warp. On the third row of weaving insert the rag, close the shed, and beat the rag down gently; open the shed and carefully lay in the fur strips on top of the rag weft, overlapping short pieces slightly so that, when the shed is closed, the fur strips are so close together that none of the rag is visible. If the rag is soft enough there may be no need to crush it by beating before the fur is inserted. Close the shed and gently press the fur down in a tight horizontal position. Beat the weft down with care. Insert the beater tines between the warp ends without piercing the fur or entangling the tines in the hair. Make the weft turns with the rag carefully, so as not to pull in the widely spaced warp. Measure the first two rows of rag weft and maintain that width throughout. Allow the fur strips to overlap and cover the rag weft turns at the selvages.

Should it be evident before starting a fur rug that there is insufficient material to complete it fully, alternate the fur weft at intervals with a woolen fabric weft of contrasting or matching color. This method, in addition to its decora-

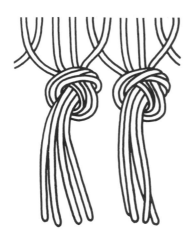

Overhand knot   Four-way braid

Rug with skidproof mesh underpad of gum and cotton

tive quality, is practical for high-pile, dense fur, such as sheepskin. It allows the pile to expand and settle under the pressure of sitting or walking. Finish the rug and cut it from the loom in stages, tying each pair of warp ends with overhand knots as they are cut from the bars. Carefully remove the stabilizing rag weft at the beginning of the weaving. Cut the second row of rag weft about 4″ from the selvage and tuck the end under the weft of the row above. Pull the warp ends back into the warp on the reverse side with a crochet hook.

FRINGES AND FINISHES

The fringe is a natural employment of the loose threads left after the warp ends have been cut from the loom. While decorative on rugs and wall hangings, fringes to some extent have a functional purpose on most floor coverings. Flat-woven rugs have a tendency to curl at the corners if left unfinished. A fringe of some substance holds the non-selvage side down. The fringe also provides a transition from the flat floor to the rise of the pile and might be considered a mini-ramp, preventing tripping over the corners. It is a traditional

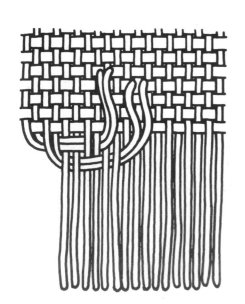

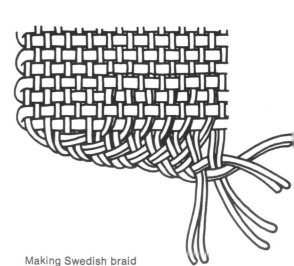

Making Swedish braid

finish, however, and might not conform to the sharp, clean lines of contemporary interiors.

There are other solutions to the problem. The Swedish braid provides a neat straight edge that is firm but still flexible. The braid can remain exposed or be turned under and hemmed to the back of the rug. About 4″ of warp are necessary for braiding. Turn the rug face down on a table and start from the left-hand side. Work with pairs of warp ends. Think of each pair of ends to be braided as the first pair in a group of four. Weave the first pair under, over, under the next three pairs. Place the end up on the body of the rug. Pick up the next pair on the left and weave it under, over, under the next three, placing the end up on the rug. Continue across the row to the right side. With each completed group of four push the braid up toward the rug, to tighten the braid and insure an even horizontal edge. Braid the last four pairs left at the right selvage, warp wrapping or whipping the ends together with a short length of matching thread. Pull the short ends back into the edge of the rug with a small crochet hook. Fold the short-end braid back and sew it to the finished braid. The braid can be a decorative edge to the finished surface, or, because of its flexibility, it can be turned under to the reverse side and invisibly hemmed. Another method for finishing the short ends, either the ends alone or with the braid turned up on the reverse side, is to cover them completely with rug seam binding. Hem the seam binding straight across the top and the bottom of the rug. Do not use seam binding on the selvages.

Saint George and the Dragon. Swedish tapestry, 1915, by Signe Asplund. Collection Gunnel Teitel

Chinese rug. Collection Edward Jamgotchian

Rug loom with woven pile rug. Courtesy Edward Jamgotchian

PILE RUGS AND WALL HANGINGS

OF ALL POSSIBLE WOVEN TEXTURES, the sensuous softness of deep pile is for many the most appealing. Whatever it may lack in sophistication for some, the allure of a full, deep velvet pile is still an expensive luxury for others, and it has been so ever since the creation of pile rugs for the pleasure of potentates in the Far East, their use as gifts to the kings and queens of Europe, and their adoption as symbols of culture and wealth among the mercantile classes everywhere.

The Oriental rugs of Chinese, Indian, and Near and Middle Eastern origins have been a creative triumph since their inception, from both the artistic and the technical point of view. There are many ways to construct a pile. Although the technique of looping was familiar to the early Greeks, the Egyptians, and the Peruvians, the Ghiordes knot and its variations, the Sehna and Spanish knots, were apparently not known or devised by them.

Over a period of time the Ghiordes knot, of Turkish origin, has become universal and diverse in its use. In England it appeared as an embroidery stitch called turkey work. Even the reverse double half hitch, the basic macramé mounting knot, is similar. A longer version formed in the same manner, called the rya or flossa knot, originated in Scandinavia. Another version popular today is constructed with the aid of a latchet hook. Each of these forms is a method for producing a thick pile suitable for rugs and for making textural additions to wall hangings.

Nineteenth-century looped pile warming cover, Crete. Detail. Collection Leon Pomerance

Oriental rug with peacocks. Collection Michael Silbert

FORMS CHARACTERISTIC OF PRAYER RUGS

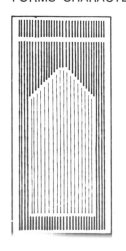

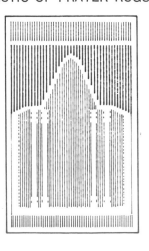

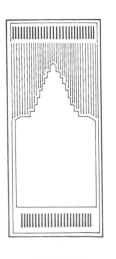

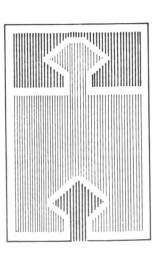

KULAH   GHIORDES   GHIORDES   BERGAMA   BERGAMA

Pile wall hanging by Sheila Hicks. Collection I. B. M. Corporation. Photo Al Mozell, Modern Masters

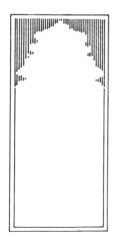

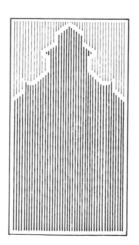

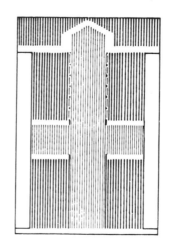

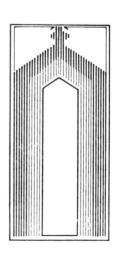

SARUK   PERSIAN   SHIRAZ   BOKHARA   BESHIR

Prayer Rug. Collection Michael Silbert

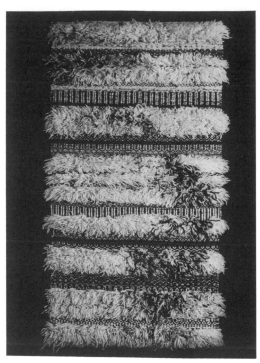

Rug by Joan Kelly Russell. Rya knotting with flat- woven bands

Caucasian rug. Collection Mr. and Mrs. Maurice Vanderwoude

Moroccan rug. Collection Mr. and Mrs. William Sadock

Entrance by Yvonne Palmer Bobrowicz

Snowscape by Collee Foster

Pile rug by Olga Fisch. Collection Michael Silbert

Swedish rug by Signe Asplund. Collection Gunnel Teitel

Rya pile rug by Edith Karlin

KNOTTED PILE

MATERIALS

Fibers used to form the pile can vary from the most beautiful silken threads to the raffia used in Hawaiian grass skirts. Any fiber that is pliable and can be turned and twisted without breaking is suitable. The traditional Oriental rug pile is composed of a single-thread knot tied around two warp threads. The warp may be of linen or cotton, and the weft knot of wool or silk.

Color choices for pile knotting can be made from among those of the same family, but of different tonal values, or among slightly different colors of similar value. The weights of the yarn can be the same or varied. A very thin yarn combined with a bulky one, plus a standard two-ply, provides variety. A fuzzy mohair may add a touch of frosting. Slight differences in the length of each strand in a single knot add texture and a shaggy touch to the over-all effect of the rug. Should there be yarns of doubtful durability, they can be used in the shorter lengths, and the longer lengths of sturdier yarns will surround and protect them from excessive wear.

RYA AND FLOSSA KNOTS

The rya knot is the same as the Ghiordes knot, but the strands are longer and the knot is often made with two or more single threads used together to form a single knot. The individual threads may vary according to color, weight, and texture. Each knot may be tied individually, using yarn cut to length in advance. This method is particularly advantageous for designs in which color changes occur frequently. Store the cut yarn in clear plastic bags according to color. To precut yarn, wind it around a guide and then cut. A 4″ × 5″ rectangle of pressed Homasote or other stiff board used as a guide for winding

Strata by Sharon Seelig. Photo Barry Seelig

and cutting will supply two different cut lengths. As the yarn is wound over and over, the length of the strips increases. Different types of yarn can be wound around the guide simultaneously, and overwound somewhat to vary the lengths. Fasten a rubber band around the center of the wound yarn to secure it in place while you cut. Cut along the top edge of the guide with a single-edged razor blade, then turn the guide over and cut the yarn across the bottom. Keep the guide with the rubber band around the middle, the razor blade stored under the band, at hand and ready for use. Cut yarn as needed.

As you work with a continuous thread, the same knots can be made linked to one another and then either cut between the links or left uncut to form a looped pile. Wind the yarn to be used for the knots into a butterfly. The length of each knot can be gauged by wrapping the links around two or three fingers according to the pile depth desired. Flossa knots are made in this way, with the length of the knots regulated by the flossa stick, a long, narrow gauge available in several widths with a groove along one side for cutting the links with a razor blade. As the knotting proceeds across the warp, the flossa stick remains in the loops, maintaining their length. Rya knots may also be woven with a continuous thread and cut later. Usually rya knots are quite a bit longer than flossa knots and are made without the use of a gauge. The knots of Oriental rugs are often regulated by a gauge stick. Of course, all knots can be sheared with scissors either as the work progresses or when the weaving is done.

WARPING A FRAME LOOM

A pile rug can easily be made on a small frame loom of any type. The warping is exactly the same as for the flat-woven rug. As the warp will be entirely covered, a strong, serviceable linen or cotton thread should be used. Plan a larger rug in small separate sections that can be added one to another as they are completed. Individually woven on a small frame, nine units, each one 18″ × 24″, could produce a rectangular rug approximately 5′ × 6′ after assembling.

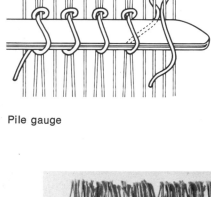

Pile gauge

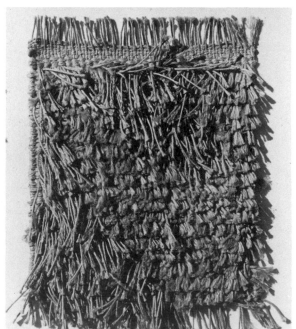

Flossa and rya knots of linen

Striped tapestry with cut looping

Frame loom with section of pile rug nearing completion

KNOTTED PILE

Each row of knots on a pile rug generally requires about ½″ of plain-weave spacing between rows so that the pile can settle when the rug is walked upon. Row upon row of Ghiordes knots produces a hard surface without buoyancy. The rows of plain weave, known as picks, or shots, of tabby between the knotted rows, hold the knots in place so that they cannot move on the warp. The color chosen for the tabby should be suited to the color of the pile. Begin the weaving with about an inch of tabby. Beat the tabby firmly, making certain that these beginning rows are horizontal and of a measured width throughout, because they form the stabilizing section of the weaving upon which the knots will rest.

THE GHIORDES OR TURKISH KNOT

The Ghiordes knot is the most common of the several types used in Oriental rugs. It is found in nearly all Turkish and Caucasian carpets and in many from Persia made by weavers of Turkish descent. Form the knot on two adjacent warp threads by placing a short piece of yarn across them and wrapping the two ends around each one. Pull the ends through the space between the two warp ends. Tie the Ghiordes knot on each pair of warp threads. Traditionally the same pair of warp threads is used for knotting on subsequent rows. Separate each row of knots with one or two rows of plain weave.

ALTERNATING GHIORDES KNOTS

An economy of wool and work is effected by skipping a warp end between knots. This is a practical approach to the spacing of rya knots where long, multiple, thicker strands are used to tie the knots. More rows of plain weave can be used because of the greater coverage given by the longer knots.

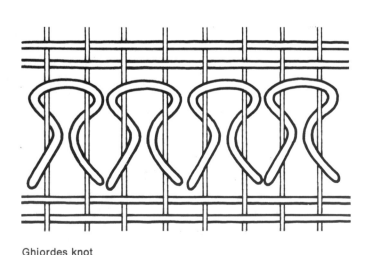

Ghiordes knot

Alternating Ghiordes knot

DIRECTIONAL GHIORDES KNOTS

The Ghiordes knot can be tied in almost any direction. Of course this is an unconventional contemporary use. Notice that the knots tied horizontally on the warp are lark's head knots.

SPANISH KNOT

The Spanish knot found in almost all Spanish pile carpets is tied around a single warp thread. Center a length of yarn over a single warp thread, cross the two ends at the back, and bring them to the front on either side of the warp thread. As this is not a true knot there is a tendency for short, individually tied knots to slip out before they are locked into place by the weft. The Spanish knot is easier to control if it is worked with a butterfly of continuous yarn rather than short lengths. Usually every other warp end is knotted. Alternate the ends to be wrapped in each row.

SEHNA OR PERSIAN KNOT

When a rug with a very fine, close pile is desired, the Sehna knot, which has only one loop turning fully around one of the pair of warp ends, permits the closer grouping of warp ends or more warp ends per inch. The yarn for the knot completely encircles one of the pair of warp-end threads emerging between the two threads, while the other end passes behind the second warp thread and emerges alongside it. The knots are maintained in successive rows on the same pairs of warp threads. One or two weft threads are used between rows. This knot is found in the majority of Persian rugs, in addition to those from Central Asia, India, and China.

Directional Ghiordes knot

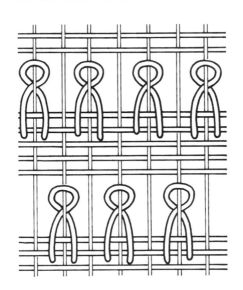

Spanish knot

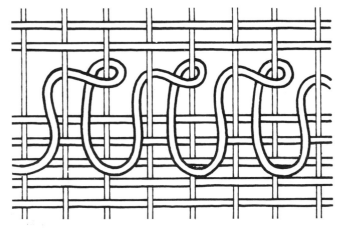

Sehna knot left

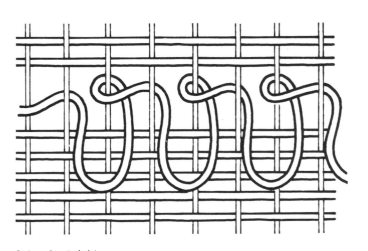

Sehna knot right

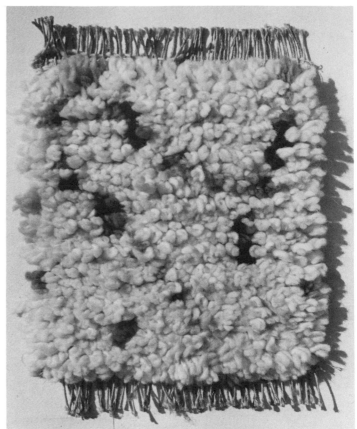

Tapestry weave with flat-woven Soumak
and directional Ghiordes knots

Flossa pile of fluffy yarn

Soumak on tapestry weave with cut loops

Looped pile and tapestry weave

Cut flossa pile

Tapestry weave with a variety of yarns
and leather knots

Cut looped pile

Tapestry weave with
leather rya pile

Weaving samples by Edith Karlin

SELVAGES

As always, the construction of the selvage must be allowed for at the beginning. Do not begin the pile at the very edge; allow at least four warp ends for building up the selvage. Even a knot of silk thread has a certain amount of height on the warp, and a rya knot composed of three or four strands may have a height of 1/4". Weave the tabby weft over and under the selvage warp ends, stopping outside the warp. The tabby weft is carried along the outside until the row of knots is completed and the next plain-weave separation begins. The selvage is worked on both the left and right side of the warp. Remember that all cut ends begin and end toward the center of the warp or a distance away from the edges. All edges are finished with weft turns.

THE WALL LOOM

A set of warp strings can be set up almost anywhere. There are some who feel that simple tools allow greater freedom. Utter simplicity in companionable surroundings can be arranged by setting up warp strings on the wall, from floor to ceiling. If there are moldings at the top and the bottom of the wall, space long nails with heads 1" apart along them. The standard rug warp is spaced 8 threads to the inch, therefore 4 warp turns around each nail will provide sufficient warp threads. Start from the bottom and make all turns in the same direction. When the warping thread is used up and more is needed, join the ends with a square knot under the bottom nail. Do not pull the warp too tightly as it must be removed from the nails at the top onto a dowel or pole, in order to provide a space between the warp and the wall for the hands to work and for the expansion of the warp as the sheds fill with weft. The best way to hold the

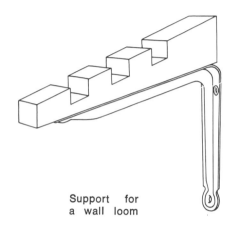

Support for a wall loom

Rug warp wound from molding to molding. Photo Curt Meinel

Rug in progress on wall loom. Photo Curt Meinel

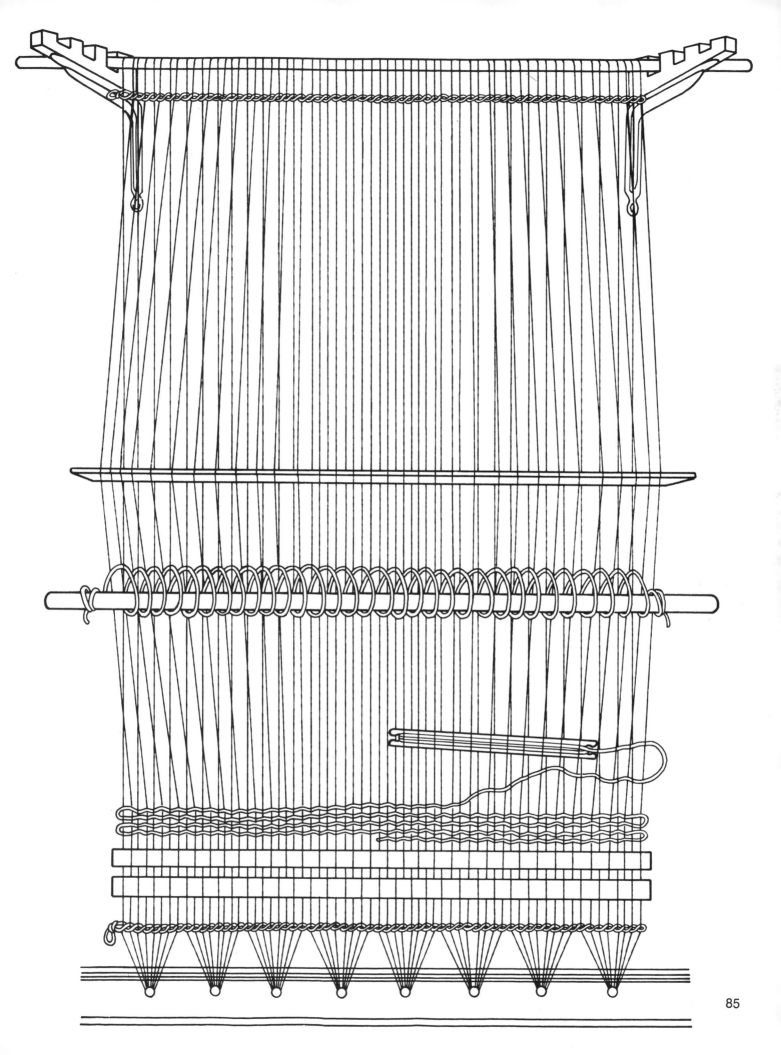

Latchet-hooked rug by Eleanor Bello

86

upper dowel away from the wall is on shelf brackets. To hold the dowel, attach a notched two-by-four to the horizontal extension of the bracket. Screw the vertical length of the bracket to the wall stud. Space the two brackets about 4′ apart. Preparation of the two-by-four is very important. The three notches, each one a step lower than the other, is a device for releasing the tension. The weaving can begin while the warp is still on the nails, but as the warp becomes too tight it must be lowered. The tightening tension becomes noticeable as the sheds become more difficult to open.

In the absence of an upper molding, screw the shelf brackets in position on the wall and warp directly around a dowel placed in the highest notch. Warping on the wall may require two people, one placing the warp over the dowel, the other receiving and turning it around the nails in the baseboard molding. If help is not available, loop the warp over the dowel and tie each pair of warp ends under the protruding nails. Spread the warp on the bottom nails by twining them apart. Insert the shed sticks and apply the heddle rod and heddles. If the heddle rod proves too cumbersome to open, as it sometimes does on long spans, use heddles in groups of nine to pull the shed open.

GLOSSARY

LATCHET HOOK
Wooden-handled straight or bent metal shank hook with a movable latchet which closes the hook over the yarn.

LARK'S HEAD KNOT
Two-stage latchet-hook knot.

RUG CANVAS
Double-thread rug canvas, preferably with twisted warp threads.

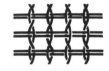

REVERSE OF LARK'S HEAD
One-stage latchet-hook knot.

LATCHET PILE

The latchet-hook method of making a knotted pile rug is a remarkably simple technique; while underrated by some weavers, it is practiced on a grand scale by others. Prominent craftsmen have a tendency to be guarded about construction, surrounding their innovations with an aura of mystery. Off-the-loom weaving as practiced in the past by many people was reintroduced in the 1960s with resounding success. Now that all the mysteries of technique are fully revealed, the clamor has subsided. But of course the craftsman is always confronted with the difficulty of creating interesting forms and successful designs. The recently expanded use of prepared canvas backings frees the weaver from the complexities of warping and puts the emphasis on designing. The ease with which knots are made with a small latchet-hook tool on a ready-made needlepoint canvas has sparked a great deal of controversy over the question of its purity as a weaving technique. In spite of the many points of view, it is comforting to remember that it is the rare painter who weaves his own canvas.

CANVAS

Double-thread cotton rug canvas for latchet hooking is available in 3 to 5 mesh intersections to 1″ in a variety of widths up to 60″. Spaced rug canvases are

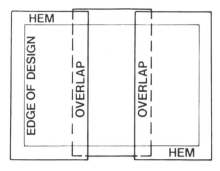

Joining short sections

HEM

EDGE OF DESIGN

OVERLAP

OVERLAP

HEM

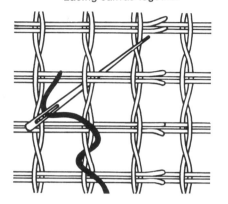

Lacing canvas together

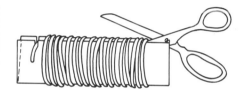

Device for cutting strips of yarn for latchet hooking

similar to those used for needlepoint. Durable canvas of desirable quality is double-threaded with a twist in the warp above and below the weft. Canvas with 4 spaces to 1″ is recommended for latchet hooking. The design must be placed on the straight of the canvas with the selvages on the right and the left. The twisted warp threads always run parallel to the selvage. The knots are placed on the weft threads.

Overlarge canvases tend to become cumbersome and heavy as the web is filled with yarn. Small sections of backing can easily be joined to make larger rugs. If the sections are too narrow, they can be joined after hooking by removing the selvages and overlapping. Allow 2″ on both edges for the overlap. Match the spaces perfectly, fitting the warp and the weft over each other exactly. Stitch the outer warp thread of the top canvas to that of the one beneath with a blunt tapestry needle and heavy thread. Repeat the stitching on the outer warp thread of the lower canvas. Overcast the warp at the mesh intersections. All knotting is done through the double layer of canvas. The slight extra thickness is durable and practically invisible under the pile.

Plan ahead if a large surface is to be worked in sections. The canvas must be large enough for the complete design and must allow for the overlap and for a sufficient border for turning a hem. Diagram the design and the overlapping edges on strips of scrap paper before cutting into the canvas. Allow a minimum of 4 or 5 spaces for the border—at least 1″—with 2″ for overlapping. Keep the selvages where possible, but cut them away on the overlap. The design will be drawn and worked on the top canvas of the overlap. Cut the canvas in the center of the weft between two parallel rows of twisted warp threads. Protect the cut ends with masking tape.

YARNS

All yarn used with the latchet hook must be cut to length in advance. The minimum length for convenient handling is 2½″. This makes a good pile about 1″ high. Precut, mothproofed yarn is available in one-ounce packets in a large variety of colors. One ounce of yarn will cover an area of approximately 4″ × 5″. Buying yarn by the pound is less expensive and it can easily be cut to any length. Prepare a guide for cutting by folding in half a piece of cardboard 2½″ × 10″. Carefully wrap the yarn around and around the length of the cardboard without overlapping. Tape the cut ends to the cardboard or make a short slit on both sides to hold the cut ends taut. Using a sharp razor blade or scissors, cut between the open edges of the cardboard. If you do a lot of this work, you may find a longer-lasting guide of Homasote or other pressed wall board more satisfactory. Yarn wound around sturdier board can be cut at both top and bottom, providing two lengths each time the yarn is wound around the guide. Cut the Homasote to the full length desired for each strip of yarn, minus ½″ to compensate for the thickness of the board. Place a rubber band around the center of the yarn before cutting. Overwinding varies the lengths of the yarn strips.

Small mechanical yarn cutters with changeable razor blades are relatively inexpensive and fun to use. These cut all pieces the same length, approximately 2½″.

A shaggy effect can be achieved without using a cutting guide. Measure ten lengths of yarn about 40″ long. Place these ten lengths across your palm, and using the width of your hand as a guide, cut the yarn into short lengths with scissors. Place all yarn pieces in clear plastic bags according to color. Textural effects change with different types of yarn. Use some yarns two at a time instead of a single strand.

THE LATCHET HOOK

Whether you choose a latchet hook with a straight or bent shank is a matter of preference; both operate on the same principle.

There are two ways to tie the latchet hook knot; either way the result is the same. Consistency is important. Experiment with both, select the method most compatible, and perfect your technique, gradually acquiring speed and evenness.

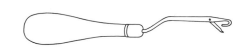

1A Fold a strip of yarn, evenly divided, around the shank of the hooker, above the handle but below the latchet.

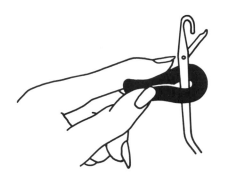

B Push the hook and latchet (with the latchet in the down position) under a weft thread and up into the space above.

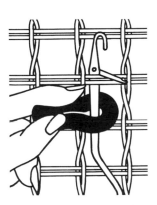

C Draw both ends evenly together, up over the latchet and under the hook. Pull the hooker back down slightly, closing the hooker.

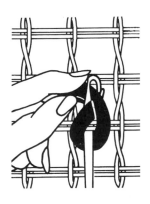

D Pull the closed hooker under the weft and through the center of the loop, releasing the ends of the yarn. Tighten the two ends around the weft.

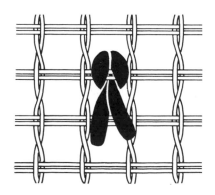

2A Push the hooker with the latchet open under the weft and up into the next space.

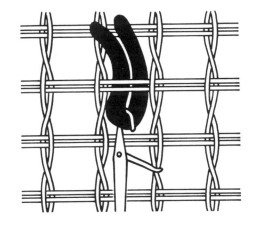

B Insert the loop of an evenly folded piece of yarn under the hook.

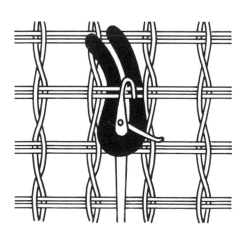

C Pull the hook and loop down under the weft. With a slight twist, push the hook farther into the loop, opening the latchet.

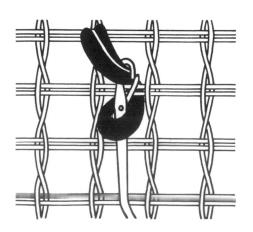

D Raise the hook upward with the loop around it, opening the latchet, and wrap the two cut ends over the shank above the latchet and under the hook.

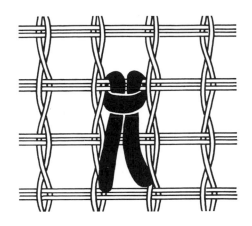

E Draw the hook down again, closing the latchet, and pull it through the loop of yarn and tighten the knot.

The knot ends will stand up as the work progresses and each space is filled. It is easiest to work upward from the bottom, adding each new row or series of knots above the other. Individual threads can be changed by pushing the pile upward, pulling out a thread, and inserting a new one.

Longer, shaggier rya knots can also be worked on canvas with a latchet hook. Three or four thinner strands of yarn grouped together and in varying lengths from 3½″ to 5″ are used for a single knot. This long, thick pile requires room for settling down. Skip one row of spaces between rows of knots. Two spaces between rows may provide a more flowing, casual effect, depending upon the type of yarn used. Intricate patterns are difficult to define with a softly flowing pile. Simple designs relying upon beautiful color for effect make the most successful rya rugs and hangings.

APPLYING DESIGNS TO CANVAS

Plan a complex design on graph paper. Consider each graph paper square as the equivalent of each canvas space. Draw and fill in the design areas on the graph paper with colored pencils, crayons, or Magic Markers. To transfer the design, mark canvas threads corresponding to the graph paper lines. Turn a crayon on its side and lightly rub it across the mesh surface to indicate color.

Simple designs, large in scale, are at their best when sketched spontaneously on a large piece of paper. Place the drawing under the canvas and transfer by marking outline indications for a broad interpretation. Large-mesh rug canvas is unsuited to minute detail. Because of the size of the mesh squares, a curve must be stepped up gradually to impart the feeling of roundness from a distance. Generally, the impact of a rug or a large wall hanging is best interpreted visually from a distance of at least 5′ away or in a general sweeping glance from even farther away.

AT THE START

Usually hemming or binding takes place when the surface has been completed. However, on rug canvases with large-mesh intersections consider turning the edges under before beginning the surface hooking. Finishing the border edges as the surface is knotted precludes adding sections to the length. Pin and stitch the top canvas to a turned-under hem of 1″ or four spaces, lining up the warp and the weft until the spaces are directly over one another. The right or left sides should be turned under only after the work at the bottom edge has been completed because of the difficulty of pulling the latchet hook through the thick overlapping at the corners of a doubled-over canvas. The knotting can start under the first weft at the edge or under the second one. If the first weft edge is left unknotted, at any time after the work has been completed an extra knot can be added, a fringe can be attached, or the edge can be finished with a row of single crocheting. An interesting facet of the single crochet is the difference in appearance between the front and the reverse side when it is used as an edging. The attractive chained braid that forms on the back makes it worth while to crochet the edge with the reverse side of the canvas facing you.

HOOKING THE DESIGN

Geometric patterns without curvilinear forms present few technical problems. Begin on the right- or left-hand side, at the bottom of the area of the canvas nearest you. Always hook the knot over the weft thread. Even after selvages have been cut away, you can identify the warp threads, which are always woven parallel to the selvages, by their twists above and below the weft. Knot across the rows, introducing new colors as needed. It is not always necessary to complete a full row before beginning the one above. It is helpful to stop the row above an unfinished one at least two or three knots short of the one below. This is particularly convenient when the colors vary from row to row. Keep a color sketch in easy view at all times. Make no attempt to finish one color at a time. Work the colors in gradually as they occur horizontally across the rows. The finished areas can rise irregularly, but knot all areas in a steady increase upward.

Latchet-hooked wall hanging by Lisa Brody

FINISHING

Backing the rug or hanging may be advisable. A backing will prevent abrasive wear that may split the knotted yarn. A latex coating is also a protection. Turn the canvas seam allowance under, stitching or adhering it to the back of the rug. Prepare a burlap or heavy linen backing 1″ larger on all sides than the rug. On wall hangings felt backing cut to size can be used. Fold back the seam allowance on the backing, mitering the corners to trim away unnecessary bulkiness. Fit to and pin the backing to the back of the rug, adjusting it carefully until the rug remains flat when turned over. Baste the backing in position. Hem the backing to the edge of the canvas mesh with linen rug-binding thread. Remove pins and basting thread.

In the absence of a backing, use binding. Choose a sturdy rug-binding tape 1½″ wide, or a width sufficient to cover the canvas mesh hem allowance. Top-stitch the binding to the front surface of the canvas mesh, as close as possible to the last row of knots. Stitch up to the first corner, then turn the binding over, bringing the reverse side up close to the knots. Stitch along this side until the next corner is reached, and repeat the turn. Turning the binding automatically miters the binding corners, and the mitering of the mesh corners as well. The mesh should be covered completely by the binding so that it becomes invisible when the binding is turned under to the back of the canvas. Trim off any excess canvas mesh, then turn and hem the binding to the back of the mesh. (See page 131.)

FRINGE

A fringe is a natural and logical finish for warp-woven rugs. The addition of fringe material to hooked pile rugs is purely decorative. You can simulate the warp ends of traditional Oriental carpets by adding a row of knots on two sides in natural linen or cotton thread. Allow one row of spaces to remain between the binding and the knots for attaching the fringe before the hem allowance is turned back. Cut and attach a few experimental knots to determine the correct length of the fringe in relation to the total size of the rug.

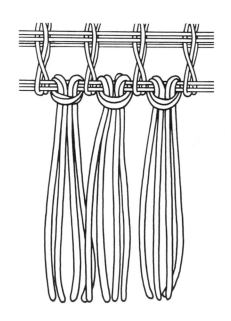

A decorative fringe of contrasting color or of a color matching the design elements, applied at either end or all around, adds to the original size of the rug. Several strips of yarn used in one knot increases fullness. Construct the fringe knot by pushing the hooker through the weft up into the space above. Grasp the loop of an evenly folded strip of yarn with the hook, pulling the loop under the weft toward you. The cut ends can be pulled through the loop with the fingers. Trim uneven ends when the fringe is completed.

RAG PILE

Young children are fascinated by this pleasant way of fabricating a pile rug. A small child can tie the Ghiordes knots along the warp threads while his mother laces together the finished knotted ropes of pile. Excitement mounts as the rug grows and grows with each row. The work can be set aside, stopped, or added to at any time. Any and every scrap of extra fiber and fabric may be used as it comes to hand to make a Hit-or-Miss pattern. Of course, all material can be saved and dyed to complement any interior or to form a colorful pattern.

Work the knots on a masonite board about 12″ × 20″, padded with an old folded bath towel or with ½″ of foam rubber covered with a small towel. The sides of the pad are laced together on the reverse side of the board. Clips, 2½″, are necessary to hold a knotting cord at the top and bottom of the padded

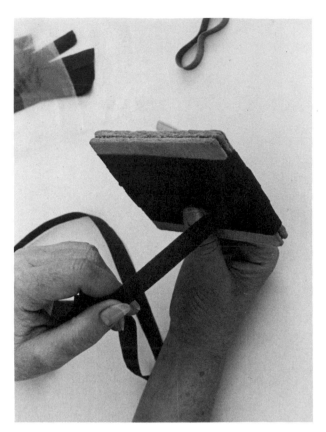
Winding rag strips on a pressed board guide

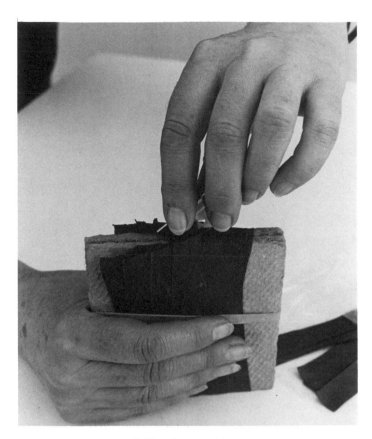
Cutting the rag strips

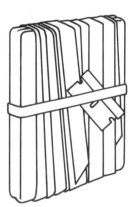

board. Use heavy three-ply jute or cotton clothesline as a warp to hold the knots. If the jute available is not thick enough to expand the knot to a fullness of at least ½", use it doubled over on itself. The knotting cord will be invisible, so perhaps other types of knotting cord will also prove suitable. Prepare strips of fabric or fiber 5" long.

The knots are tied around two cords. Cord can be added at any time, attached together with a square knot. Begin with cords of uneven length in order to stagger the square knots when additions are made. Fold a 4-yard length of cord unevenly in half. One of the cut ends should be about ½ yard shorter than the other. Place the loop of the uncut end in the center of the knotting board, dropping the extra yardage over the top of the board. Place the clip over the two cords at the top of the board to hold them firmly in place. Center a strip of the prepared knotting material across both cords. Using both hands, hold the cut ends between the thumb and index fingers. Spread the cords apart with the thumb and third finger of one hand and draw the two cut ends between the cords, down to the end of the loop. Tighten the knot. Place several more knots above the first one before pulling the looped end down to the bottom of the board. Clip it to the board at the bottom, straightening and readjusting the cords until they are tightly clipped at the top. Always keep the right-hand cord on the right. Do not allow the cords to reverse their positions by twisting around. Release the clip and move the boa of knots down on the board as they are completed, maintaining a comfortable working area near the center of the board.

Knot several yards of cord before attempting to form a rug. An oval is simple to construct, using a straight, doubled 9" length of the knotted cord as the center. Double the entire cord. Using the doubled end as the rug's 9" center, wind the doubled cord around and around, forming an oval. With large needles

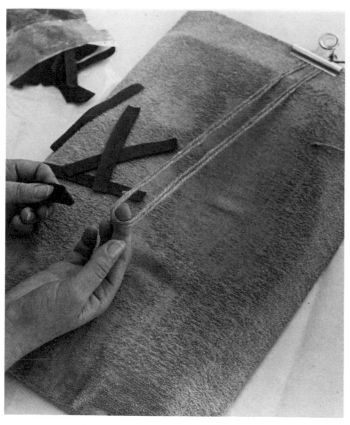

Starting a rag-pile rug on jute cords

Tieing the Ghiordes knot

The beginning knot

Continuous knotting on padded board

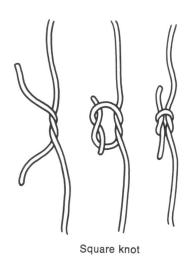

Square knot

and heavy linen rug-binding thread, lace the outer coil of one pair of cords to the inner cord of the next pair in a figure eight. Starting at the approach to the curve, ease the curves in during lacing by narrowing the space between the lacing turns on the inner coil while broadening the spaces along the outer coil. As the rug becomes heavier and larger in size, keep it on the floor at your feet, separately preparing additional lengths to lace around the growing perimeter without disturbing the knotting on the board.

The square knot is the secret to the successful joining of vertical threads. Add a new warp cord early enough to enclose the short ends of warp in the rag knotting. Place the new cord alongside the old one, cut ends up and level. Hold each end between thumb and index finger 2½″ down from the top, and tie as follows:

Left over right, down, around, and up.

Right over left, around and through.

Avoid excessive knotting of the warp cords after the starting loop by working from two separate balls of cord, one feeding the right side, the other the left side.

This technique can be worked with heavy rug yarn in a combination of fabric and yarn in alternating rows. Latex applied to the back of the rug will prevent undue abrasion on the lacing thread.

Starting an oval

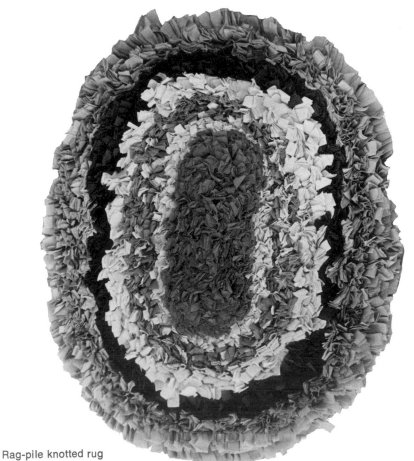

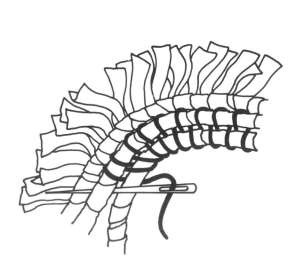

96   Easing a curve   Rag-pile knotted rug

2

3

4

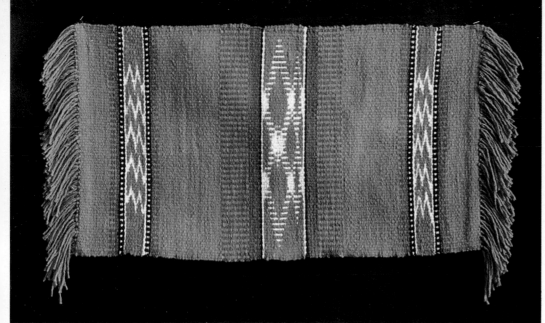

5

6

7

9

0

10

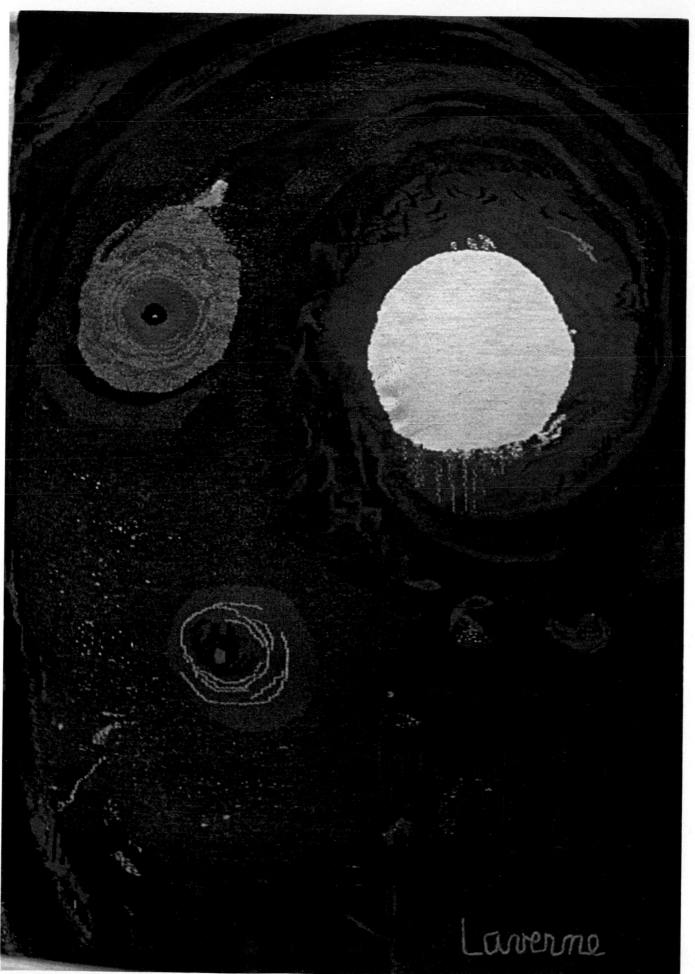

11

12

13

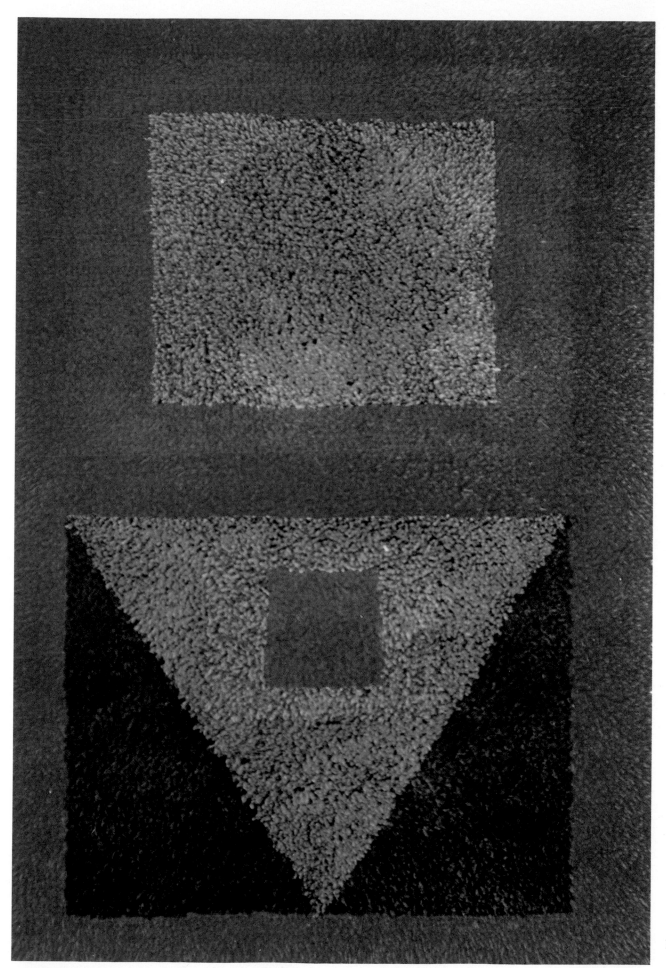

14

16

17

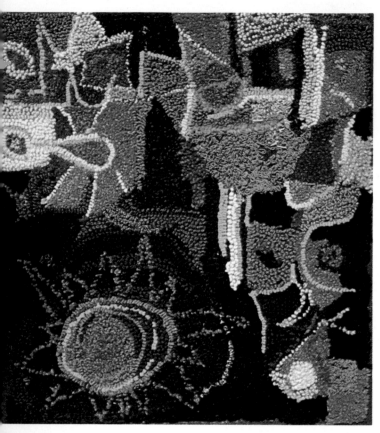

18

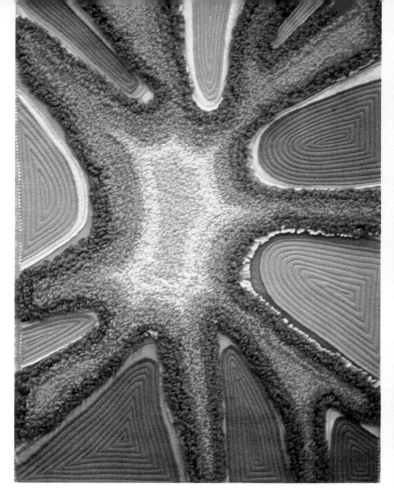

19

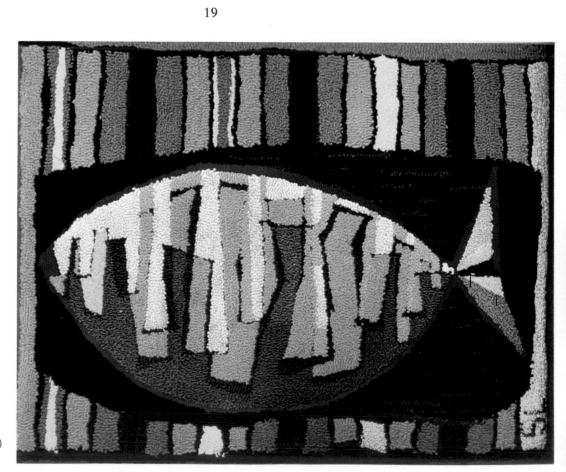

20

23

24

25

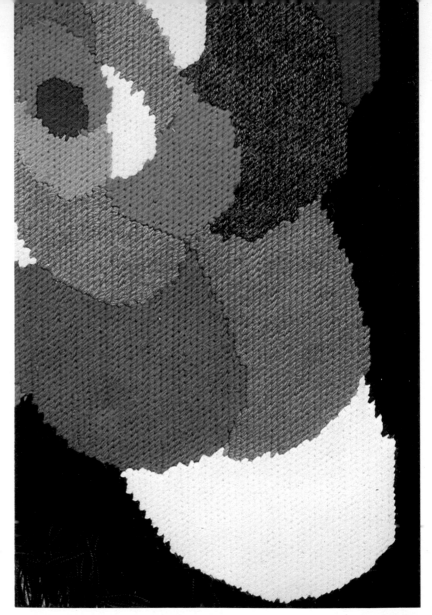

27

26

28

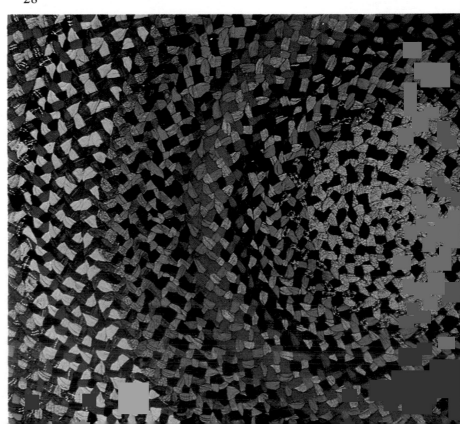

29

30

31

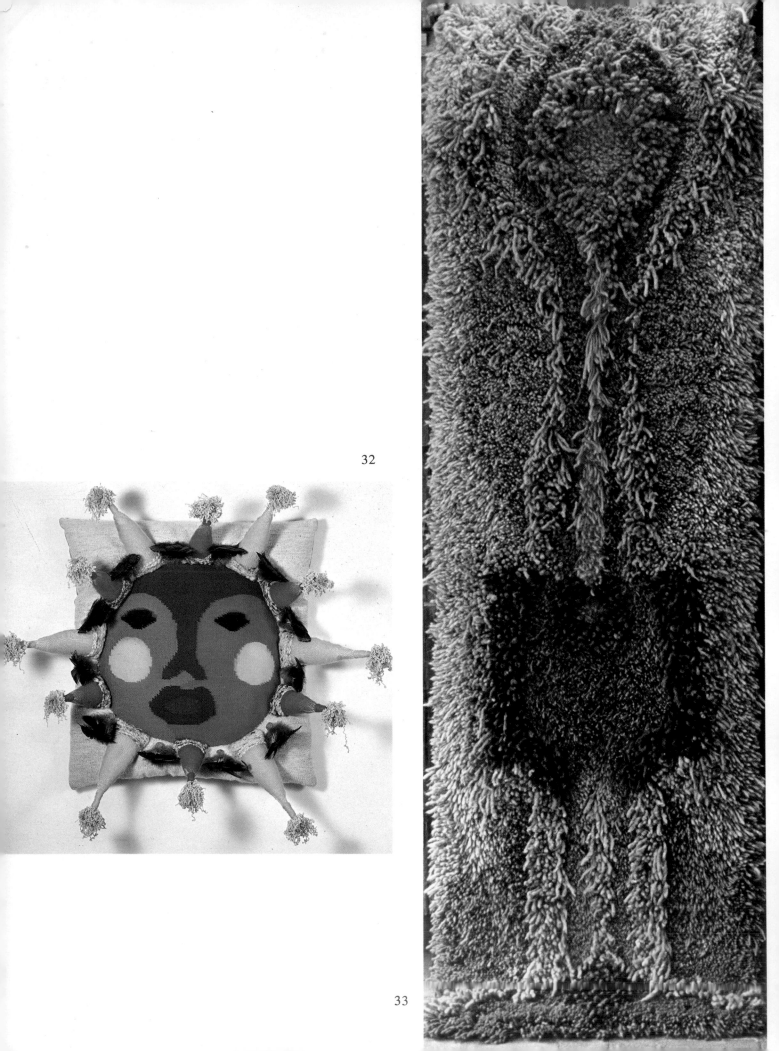

32

33

1. *Jewel* by Brenda Le Poidevin. Woven wool with the addition of macramé. Collection Canadian Guild of Crafts

2. Round frame-loom hanging worked on vertical warp with edging of Soumak by Frances Wong

3. *Pillow Sacks* by Roger Oates. Photo David Jones Evans

4. Woven wall hanging by Robert Mabon

5. Weft-faced Ikat rug, vegetable-dyed. Rochester Folk Art Guild

6. *Courting Grouse,* woven and hooked wall hanging by Brenda Le Poidevin

7. Tapestry wall hanging by Irja Mikkola

8. After *Every Third* by Kenneth Noland. Tapestry in hooked-rug technique. Courtesy Pace Editions, Inc.

9. Dubrovnik. Woven tapestry by Gabriella Hajnal

10. After *Flin Flon XIII 1970* by Frank Stella. Flat woven tapestry. Courtesy Pace Editions, Inc.

11. Tapestry woven by Sally Shore after a painting by Erwine Laverne

12. Rya rug by Melissa Cornfeld

13. *Symphony* by Collee Foster. Flat weaving with knotting

14. *Triangle.* Knotted rug by Irja Mikkola

15. *Red Arrow.* Flat-woven wall hanging with knotting by the author

16. Hooked rug by Helen Jacoff

17. Latchet-hooked wall hanging by Lisa Brody

18. Hooked wall hanging of fabric and yarn by Muriel Zimmerman

19. Felt appliqué and hooked rug by Vesta B. Ward

20. *Fish* by Shirley Lewin. Hooked wall hanging

21. *The Three Kings* by the author. Hooked and embroidered wall hanging, with macramé

22. *Landscape* by Lisa Brody. Latchet-hooked wall hanging

23. Hooked wall hanging of fabric and yarn by Muriel Zimmerman

24. Hooked circular design by Sally Shore inserted in broadloom rug

25. Crocheted rug. Rochester Folk Art Guild

26. Crocheted rug

27. Needlepoint rug by Dr. Isadore Epstein

28. Braided rug by Virginia Seelig. Photo Barry Seelig

29. Wall hanging by Barbara Bonisteel. Macramé and weaving on a frame loom. Courtesy Canadian Guild of Crafts

30. Wall hanging by the author

31. Rya turkey-work rug

32. Woven pillow by Sharon Seelig

33. Rug by the author. Embroidered turkey-work of Mexican homespun wool

Early-nineteenth-century American hooked rug. Collection Mr. and Mrs. Sydney Jacoff

Owl. American hooked rug of the early nineteenth century. Collection Mr. and Mrs. Sydney Jacoff

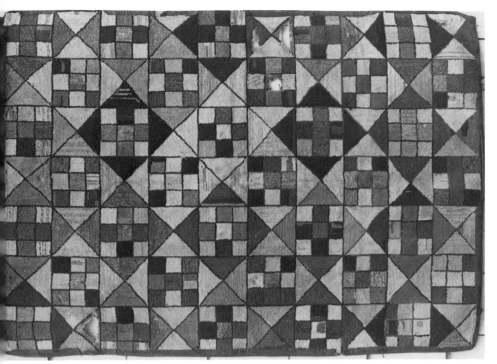

Patchwork-design American hooked rug. Collection Mr. and Mrs. Edmund Marein

HOOKED RUGS AND WALL HANGINGS

THE CRAFT OF RUG HOOKING has always been an art of the people, popular among farm wives in isolated villages, fishermen and sailors with many idle hours, or ladies wishing to pursue a genteel art. European in origin, the technique most likely was inspired by the looping evident in Coptic weaving. Some of the earliest known remnants of hooking, dating from the Bronze Age, have been found in Danish and Norwegian tombs. These fragments were intended for use as bedding, as were later examples found in northern Ireland, Scotland, Wales, and northern England. In the early days of hand spinning and weaving, cloth was a precious possession in England and on the Continent. Clothing was worn, cut, and resewn, passed down from one member of the family to the next until it was so worn that it was irretrievable. Every scrap and remaining useful portion of fabric was washed, the seams opened, and the cloth set aside for further use by thrifty householders. The ragbag provided a supply of materials close at hand for patchwork quilts and rag rugs. A bare English cottage with no other carpets might have a small hearth rug contributing additional cheerfulness to the warmth of the fireside.

These early rag rugs were sometimes referred to as brodded or pegged rugs because of the method used in inserting the strips of cloth into the backing fabric. A brod was a round-headed nail made by a blacksmith and was used to prick or prod holes in the backing cloth. A wooden peg was also used in the same manner. The end of a short, rectangular strip of cloth was pushed through one hole, and the other end was pushed through another hole close to the first one. Both cut ends were pulled up taut on the right side. The short tufts which composed the surface of the rug were then sheared, if necessary, to an even height.

Each member of the family and every family in the town was employed in the fabrication of cloth for domestic use, as well as for export. Piecework for the industry was performed by a great many people who worked at home. The term "cottage industry" derives from this period. After completed weaving is cut from a loom, modest lengths of unwoven warp remain tied to the front and back beams of the loom. These waste warp ends are called thrums. It is quite

Detail of multicolored floral runner. Collection Mr. and Mrs. Andrew Geller

likely that the impoverished cottage industry worker saved and accumulated the warp ends, utilizing the shortest ends in the same manner as the cloth scraps. The longer lengths of yarn were pulled up through the cloth backing, often an open-weave sacking of the type used for produce bags, in a succession of loops. Short loops were left standing close to the cloth surface or trimmed to an even height. Most of these looped fabrics were used as coverlets and called bed rugs. It is interesting to note the Scandinavian origin of the word "rug" and to compare it with the Norwegian forms, *rugga* or *rogga,* meaning a coarse coverlet.

The Pilgrims set sail for the new world with their most valued and useful possessions, including bedding and bedclothes. Bedclothes consisted of voluminous draw drapes used on the beds of that period for warmth and privacy. The journey from Europe was strenuous, and the nine months after dropping anchor off Plymouth in November 1620 had to be spent on the *Mayflower* while stockades and rude shelters were built. The brutal winter months were filled with uncertainty and distress. Food was scarce, and the only real warmth and comfort was probably provided by the bedding brought from Europe.

The early settlers in America were a diverse group of dissidents, for the most part from urban areas, unaccustomed to providing elementary essentials for themselves. The development of linen from flax seeds to thread is a lengthy process consuming the better part of sixteen months. Establishing suitable conditions for the grazing and breeding of sheep was as difficult for the settlers as was the processing of the wool. The settlers used whatever cloth was brought with them until they became more firmly established. Although a great deal of weaving, including the spinning and dyeing of fibers, was done at

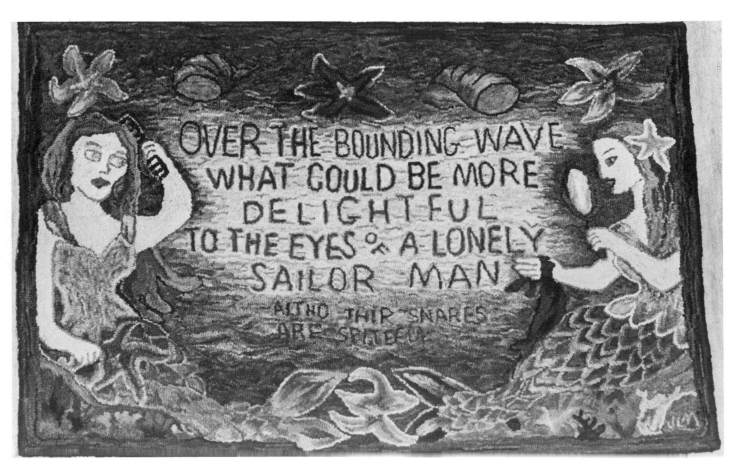

The Mermaids by Joan Moshimer. Inspired by an early-American hooked rug which was probably made by a sailor

Brick-pattern American hooked rug. Collection Mr. and Mrs. Edmund Marein

Hooked rug. Collection Mr. and Mrs. Sydney Jacoff

Early-American hooked rug with leaf-scroll border. Collection Mr. and Mrs. Sydney Jacoff

117

Hooked rug of multicolored wool scrap material. Early American. Collection Mr. and Mrs. Sydney Jacoff

home, still itinerant weavers were hired to supplement family labor and meet the pressing need for cloth of all kinds. Almost immediately it became apparent that professional weavers were needed. Before the middle of the seventeenth century families of clothmakers from the English Midlands were brought to Massachusetts. Cottage industries similar to those in England became the nucleus of the New England textile industry.

The transitional period, between the time when the construction of rugs for bed and table covers was all done at home and the advent of steam-operated carpet looms, was extremely short. Occasionally, affluent and more style-conscious families might use hand-painted or stenciled designs on canvas as floor coverings. However, the use of rag carpets made from scraps salvaged from

Basket of roses. Collection Mr. and Mrs. Andrew Geller

Floral rag rug hooked in an adaptation of an early-American design. Collection Mr. and Mrs. Edmund Marein

Early hooked runner in floral design. Collection Mr. and Mrs. Sydney Jacoff

old clothing or from pieces left over from the cutting of new clothing was most prevalent in the average home. Homespun linen often served as a base for hooked rugs, although burlap and other sacking materials were more common. Many of the early patterns made by rural people were simple stripes or designs based on the geometric shapes innate in patchwork. At the same time florals and scrolls reminiscent of Tudor England appeared on hooked-rug designs copied from embroidered bedclothes. English crewel-embroidery designs of the period are based on a highly sophisticated combination of Indian and Persian art forms, as well as on a love of the flowers of the English garden. As many early-American hooked rugs were based on themes of fruit and flowers as were based on Hit-or-Miss patterns that utilized odds and ends of scrap

Hooked rug. Collection Mr. and Mrs. Andrew Geller

material. Other subject matter might be Biblical. The Peaceable Kingdom was a favorite. Just as popular then as they are today were commemorative themes —the homestead, a favorite dog or cat, heraldic symbols, marriages and anniversaries. The itinerant craftsman, the artistic counterpart of the country peddler, sought work in all rural areas. The limner painted portraits, others painted tavern signs, and by the early nineteenth century painted burlap canvases copied from prize-winning hooked rugs exhibited at county fairs were offered for sale. These popular patterns found ready acceptance, and the craft itself became widespread, gaining mass appeal. To some extent the unself-conscious freedom to create was forever lost, at least for the quiet and the shy, the naïve and the primitive.

GLOSSARY

STRAIGHT HOOK
All-purpose tool with straight shank and wooden handle. Pulls loops up to the top surface.

BENT HOOK
All-purpose tool with a bent shank and wooden handle. Pulls loops up to the top surface.

HOOKED LOOPS

Loops pulled to the surface with straight or bent shank hooker.

PUNCH NEEDLE
Adjustable punch needle, for moderately paced speed hooking. Pushes the loops down from the back of the fabric.

SHUTTLE HOOKER
Adjustable shuttle hooker with wooden handles for fast speed hooking.

SPEED TUFTER
Another type of adjustable speed hooker.

YARN PAINTER
Electric speed hooker.

PUNCHED LOOPS
Loops pushed down from the back of the fabric with punch needles and speed hookers.

Hooked rugs have come a long way since the eighteenth century—all the way from pulling the loops up to pushing the loops down, made with anything from a bent nail to an electrified hooker. In each method the craftsman faces the design drawn on the foundation fabric. When the loops are pulled up, the finished design appears on this surface. When the loops are pushed downward with a punch needle, the finished surface is on the opposite side of the fabric; therefore the design should be reversed before it is traced on the fabric. Pulling up the loops from underneath is a slower method of construction, but the pleasure of watching the finished surface develop and expand across the foundation fabric is rewarding. Each loop is controlled by hand and regulated by eye. With experience, one develops the ability to judge the height of the pile, and within a short time this ability becomes fairly automatic. Punch needles and shuttle hookers have adjustments for controlling the height of the looped pile. Pre-setting the desired height allows long rows of hooking to be worked rapidly. Because the punch needle pushes the loops downward, the underside of the rug is the foundation fabric facing you. As the work progresses, the right side must be viewed now and then to see how the effect of the finished surface is progressing. Cloth strips work well with either method. However, extra care should be taken not to split yarn when pulling it up from the underside with a hook. Punch and shuttle hookers easily accommodate a wide variety of yarn sizes. Wide strips of cloth, unspun or novelty yarn, or usual weights of yarn, cable cords, jute, and sisal are best pegged and pushed, or else pulled through the foundation fabric with a hook. Combinations of techniques, such as hooking and embroidery, may be worked on both sides of the foundation fabric.

Hooked rug in hand-dyed yarns by George Wells. Design suggested by the legend of the New Jersey Revolutionary War heroine who hid her horse from the British in her home in Morristown, New Jersey. Collection of the present Miss Tempe Wick

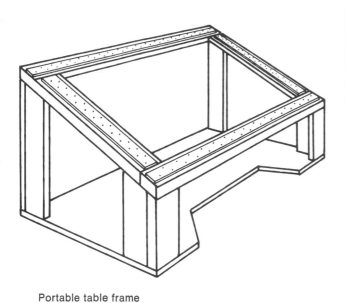

Portable table frame

Duraback stretched on a rug-hooking frame

HOOKING FRAME

A stretched, taut foundation fabric is the most comfortable and workable surface for hooking. Although a small sample piece or a pillow top could possibly be worked without a frame, working on an artist's canvas stretcher or an empty picture frame is easier and produces more even work. Stretcher strips and picture frames are not practical for making rugs and wall hangings of any reasonable size.

Adjustable frames on legs with a top that can be tilted are available in a variety of widths from manufacturers or school and craft suppliers. Some commercial frames have a turning device for rolling up the unused and the finished portions, but these can hold only a limited amount of the finished part of a rug with a thick pile. Certain frames with legs can be folded flat with the half-completed work on them for storing.

A portable table frame designed for pulling up the loops with a hook can be handmade of 1″ × 2″ lumber and plywood. The side and bottom openings leave room for holding the strips of yarn or fabric under the foundation fabric. Cover the top edges of the frame with tackless carpet stripping (which can be purchased from stores that sell and install broadloom carpet). You can work sections of the rug anywhere on the foundation fabric by stretching the fabric over the tack heads of the stripping and moving it to a new section as each one is finished. Many rug hookers place a felt strip over the tack heads where they emerge though the foundation fabric, to protect their hands and arms.

Many economical craftsmen prefer to build practical, sturdy frames that can be placed on sawhorses and worked from a sitting position or used tilted against a wall. Lumber selected for the four sides of the frame should be strong and free of large knots, especially near the center, to eliminate warping and the possibility of breaking under tension. (A foundation fabric is most satisfactory when stretched almost as tight as a drum.) The inside dimension of the frame should be 1½″ wider all around than the width of the finished rug, in order to have room to work along the edges with accuracy and comfort. An ideal size for a 20″ × 30″ hearth rug would be a workable interior size of 23″ × 33″. If 1½″ lumber was used, the exterior size would measure 26″ × 36″. Although the weight of the lumber for this small size may seem excessive, it provides the height necessary to accommodate the downward thrust of the hooker, in addition to being indestructible even when used over and over again.

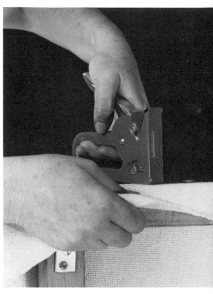

Portable cloth hooking frame.
Courtesy Dolores Wiemann

Angle irons in position on a handmade frame

Stapling the stretched canvas

At least 2″ of the excess backing fabric, after it has been removed from the frame, is used for turning under and hemming the edges of the completed rug or wall hanging.

Lumber of this weight can be utilized for almost any rug width. For sizes of more than 5′ it is sensible to add a vertical center support that can be moved to the right or left, out of the way, when you are working in the center of the rug. Cut the top and bottom pieces long enough to fit across the ends of the vertical members of the frame. Although the frame will be turned on its side some of the time, this arrangement provides greater strength during most of the hooking on a frame used leaning against a wall. Reinforce the frame corners with angle irons in the inside, and with flat L-shaped angles on the surface.

Fabric for modest sizes can be attached to the frame with thumbtacks, carpet tacks, or a staple gun. Larger sizes should be attached in a manner that is easily adjustable. As the hooking proceeds, working pressure and the weight of the pile lessen the tension, requiring the restretching of parts every so often. Tackless carpet stripping nailed to the surface of the frame will work well with medium-size pieces, but larger ones are often stretched over 3″ finishing nails hammered into the surface of the frame every 2½″. These headless nails are left upright, protruding about 1¼″ from the frame.

FOUNDATION FABRIC

A backing fabric is suitable for hooking when the warp and the weft are even and apparent. Two-ply monk's cloth is a serviceable white cotton rug backing. Duraback, a single-ply, firmly woven, white cotton canvas, is excellent for both rugs and wall hangings. Its rugged, heavy texture is good looking when left exposed, and at the same time its particular construction lends itself to work done in combined techniques. Duraback can be dyed. Both monk's cloth and duraback can be purchased in a variety of widths up to 16′. The least expensive backing, often used in schools, is burlap, but any even-weave cotton or fabric of linen fiber is preferable to the rough jute of burlap. There are jute and jute-blend fabrics that are commendable. However, the inexpensive burlap generally used in schools is uneven in weave, and the fibers are

123

easily broken and will not wear well, particularly when subject to friction and dampness. Burlap becomes brittle with age and is difficult to repair.

After cutting the fabric, tape all raw edges with masking tape to prevent unraveling. The edges could also be secured with an overhand stitch or with a large running stitch made on the sewing machine. Allow at least 2″ of margin all around the design area for hemming, plus an extra 2″ for attaching to the frame.

ATTACHING FABRIC TO FRAME

Always try, if possible, to place the fabric on the frame so the selvages will be on the left and right sides as the work progresses. All fabric is woven on a taut warp. The weft is woven from left to right, with selvages on either side. Fabric will stretch more through the weft, or from left to right. Having the selvages at the sides, rather than the ends, helps to maintain a straight and even edge as you work, especially when a lining fabric is used in conjunction with the upper surface. Fold the fabric in half, then in half again, marking each center point. It is extremely important that the warp and weft be kept at right angles to each other. Using a felt-tipped marker, draw a line through the horizontal weft threads where they will be attached to the frame. Starting from the centerfold mark, attach one side of the fabric to the frame at a time. A few thumbtacks placed at intervals help to keep it in place for final tacking. Staple small pieces of fabric backing, or use carpet tacks. Do not push or hammer tacks all the way in until all adjustments have been completed. If finishing nails are used instead of tacks, place the fabric over the nails carefully so that neither the warp nor the weft fibers of the fabric are split. Place the fabric over the finishing nail in the space at the right angle between the warp and the weft. Arrange the other three sides at the center points, pulling each straight and taut with the warp and the weft. Pushing the finishing nail slightly toward the outsides of the frame will tighten the fabric when necessary.

Hooking a large canvas stretched on a frame loom

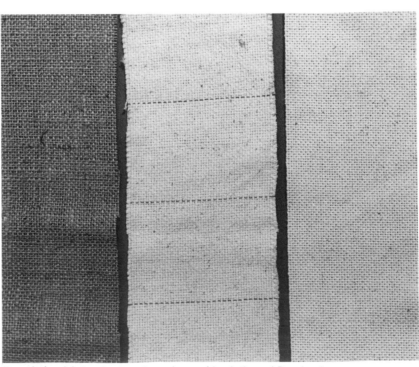

Foundation fabrics: burlap, two-ply monk's-cloth, and Duraback

If you plan to use seam binding to finish the edges of the rug, it is sometimes convenient to apply the binding to the foundation before hooking the rug. This is practical only on rugs constructed by pulling up the loops with a hook because pulling applies less pressure on the tautly stretched foundation fabric than punch needles and shuttle hookers. Extra fabric should extend beyond the seam binding, to be trimmed narrower than the binding when the rug is finished.

Commercial frames for hooking have a front and a back beam for rolling and storing the backing fabric. A narrow working area of about 20" is left after the backing fabric is rolled on. The widths may vary from 20" to 60". Obviously the design must be applied to the fabric before the fabric is attached to the frame. Tack the fabric to the upper or top crossbeam with thumbtacks, starting from the center and working to the left and the right. Tack in a straight line between two parallel weft threads. Begin an inch or two away from the side stretcher. Roll the backing fabric over and around the upper crossbeam until only enough fabric is left to cover the span between the upper crossbeam and the lower crossbeam. Turn slowly, making certain that the fabric is rolling on evenly. It is helpful to have someone standing at the front of the frame holding the width of the fabric outstretched with two hands while the upper crossbeam ratchet is turned. Attach the other end to the lower crossbeam with thumbtacks. Roll the fabric toward you around the lower crossbeam until the beginning of the design is in position, ready to work, and the fabric is taut.

An apron of strong canvas attached to the upper and lower crossbeams eliminates the need to tack the backing fabric to the beams each time a new rug backing is rolled on the frame. Sometimes the crossbeams are cut from very hard wood, making it very difficult to push in thumbtacks. In that case construct two short canvas aprons, each about 8" long and as wide as the beams. Staple the aprons to the beams with a large household staple gun of the type used for installing insulation, then sew the backing fabric to the aprons. Overlap about 2" of the backing fabric on the apron. Hold the two pieces in place with straight pins. Using long back stitches, sew across the width. Roll the fabric onto the beams. The right and left sides must be pulled taut. Thread a large-eyed needle with strong thread or cord and tie the end around the side stretcher. Lace the fabric to the side stretcher in a spaced figure eight. Lacing of this kind must be cut from the frame as each section of the work is completed, and the backing fabric must be moved forward. Another method of pulling the sides taut is to insert T pins lengthwise along the sides of the backing fabric about every two inches. Draw the lacing cord from the side stretcher and wind it around the head of the pin and under the point projecting from the fabric, then back and around the side stretcher. When the T pins are removed, the lacing cord will fall free. Do not distort the fabric by pulling and lacing it on the bias; always remember to keep the weft running from left to right in a straight line. The advantage of the adjustable roll-on frame is that one can sit close to the work. However, the bulk of the design and the finished portion is rolled up and out of sight on the beams as you work. The entire design and color field cannot be continuously viewed, considered, and adjusted, so it is advisable to have a completed color rendering to follow.

TRANSFERRING THE DESIGN

On flat frames (without rollers) the design can be applied before or after stretching the backing fabric. The choice will depend upon the type of stretcher used and the experience of the craftsman. Place the small unstretched fabric on a flat surface and tack or tape it down to prevent any movement. Pin or tape the design to it, with carbon paper between the design and the fabric. Trace over the design with a ball-point pen. If the transferred design is weak, work over the lines with a felt-tipped marker. Larger drawings involving simple forms can be rendered on wrapping paper, then cut out in sections. Each separate section can be pinned to the backing fabric and outlined with a marker. Moderate-size drawings can be scaled to size with a grid. With a pencil, divide the original drawing into equal quarters, then divide each section in quarters again. There will be sixteen sections. The background fabric must be in the same proportion as the drawing. For instance, if the drawing is 9″ × 12″, the backing fabric for the enlargement should be in direct relationship to that size. Four times 9″ × 12″ would be 36″ × 48″, an enlarged size directly related to the original drawing. To this enlargement you must, of course, add extra measurements needed for finishing the edges. Divide and section the backing fabric in the same manner as the drawing. Transfer the design, drawing one section at a time.

Another method for transferring a design is with an opaque projector. Attach the fabric to a wall with masking tape. Focus the projector on the fabric surface, and outline the projected image with a felt-tipped marker. An enlargement can easily be made with a photostat. Remember that punch and shuttle hooking is worked from the back; therefore the design should be reversed before it is traced. This point is critical when lettering or numbers are an integral part of the design. Coloring the areas on the backing fabric with crayons is a helpful guide, although crayons can only indicate areas of color and can never match the variety or beauty of dyed yarns.

HOOKERS FOR YARN AND CLOTH

Every rugmaker has a favorite hooker. Odd as it may seem, it appears there are also regional favorites. The Montell hooker, now known as a Speed Tufter, is well known and used extensively on the West Coast, as is the Yarn Painter, an electrified automatic puncher. Both have a pile range of approximately ⅛″ to 1½″. Hooking devices familiar to rugmakers in the eastern United States include a wide range of punch needles and shuttle hookers. The punch needle

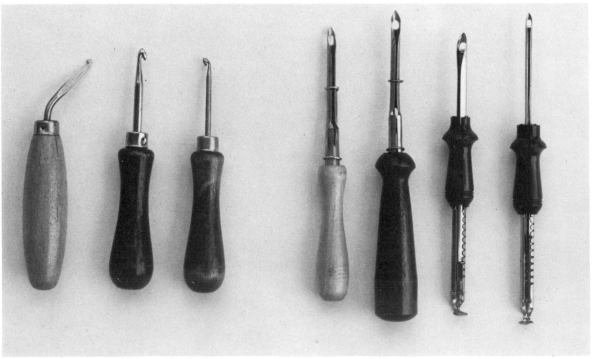

Cloth hookers and punch needles

has a single point that pushes the yarn through the back of the foundation fabric and is carefully withdrawn, leaving a loop on the right side. The yarn and punch needle point must be moved along the fabric without disturbing the length of the loop on the underside. The punch needle is held in one hand in the same manner one would hold a pencil.

Simple punch needles have a limited loop length. The Columbia Minerva punch needle has two interchangeable points and adjusts to ten different loop lengths, from 3/8" to 7/8". All punch needles are easy to work with one hand while seated.

The shuttle hooker is constructed in two moving parts. The needle point pierces the fabric while the flat looper pushes the loop a specific length down through the fabric. At the same time the needle point is drawn up and advances to the next loop position.

The use of shuttle hookers requires both hands, and although it is possible to adjust to working from a sitting position, operation is less awkward when one is standing. Better suited to rags than yarn is the Susan Burr shuttle hooker with a single loop length of about 3/8". More versatile is the sturdy Tru-Gyde shuttle hooker, with interchangeable points and loopers in two sizes. Both needle sizes will take yarn and rags, although the rags for the smaller of the two needles must be cut narrowly. The smaller needle has four settings, from 1/4" to 7/8"; the larger needle three settings, from 3/8" to 3/4". The Paterna rug-tufter can be adjusted to a very deep rya pile of almost 3". Shuttle hookers cover areas much faster than the punch hook, but the speed makes them somewhat less accurate. Both types are worked from the reverse side of the fabric.

YARNS

Naturally, everyone wants a rug that is long-wearing, mothproof, and resilient; therefore consider purchasing the best possible rug yarn. The very best yarns are well spun and smoothly finished. For both rugs and wall hangings firm, thick rug yarns in three or four plys, of heavy, medium, or fine weights, are

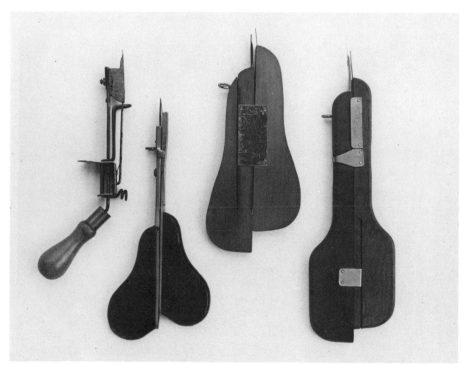

Speed shuttle hookers

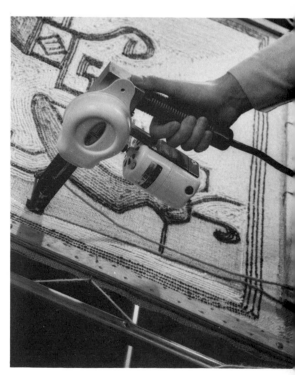

Electric speed hooker. Courtesy Yarn Painter

Floral medallion with sea-shell border in a rug hooked by Helen Jacoff

Hooked rug by Virginia Pedulla

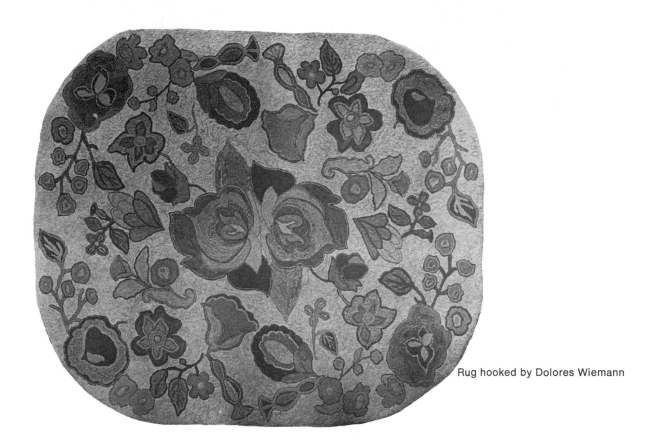

Rug hooked by Dolores Wiemann

Landscape by Lola Sherwin. Hooked wall hanging in blues, greens, and white

most satisfactory. Knitting yarn is too stretchy. As the yarn must run freely through the punch and shuttle hookers, yarn that thins out and separates is annoying to use, nubby novelty yarns have a tendency to jam the hooker, and heavy, almost felted yarns, such as Mexiskein, are not suitable. A good many carpet manufacturers today use yarns of man-made fibers. These synthetic yarns are much less costly than woolen yarn and quite satisfactory for hooking.

The traditional, truly hooked rug is worked with a small wooden-handled crochet hook with which one pulls the loops through the fabric to the top. These are available in several sizes and shapes. A large one is made for use with wide, heavyweight rags and loose, shaggy yarn. Medium hooks are for general work and can be purchased with a bent or straight shank. The very small hooks are suitable for very fine work. It is customary to use fine woolen fabric strips with this traditional hooking tool.

PREPARING WOVEN FABRICS FOR HOOKING

The ragbag is a ready source of materials but is by no means inexhaustible. Thrift shops, bazaars, and firms specializing in mill ends are additional sources. All fabrics must be clean before they are stored or prepared for use. Although most fabrics are preshrunk, it is best to wash old clothing to eliminate sizing and to shrink woolens. Loose weaves benefit from shrinking even if matting occurs. There is then less danger of the loose weave pulling apart when cut fine. The tighter the weave, the thinner the strips can be cut. Open all seams. Remove buttons, zippers, pockets, collars, linings, and other stiffeners; cut away weak spots, moth damage, and obvious disfiguring stains. Sort rags according to the material content. Almost any kind of material can be used: woolens, cotton, silk, knitted tricots; synthetics such as nylon, Dacron, rayon, and other acrylic fibers. However, woolens of medium weight are the most desirable for a serviceable rug. A tightly woven 100 per cent wool flannel is widely used. Mixing materials of different content should be avoided, because some fibers do not wear as well as others and are not as resistant to soil. Woolen yarn can be used to advantage with woolen rags. Sort the rags again, separating the tweeds and plaids from the solid colors. Solid colors can be

Preparing cloth with a strip cutter

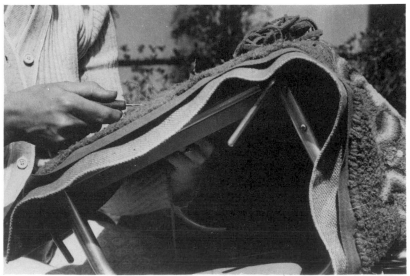

Positioning the cloth strips for hooking

divided into light, medium, and dark tonal groups. The tweeds and plaids produce unique patterns through the admixture of diverse broken color. Dyeing the fabrics should be considered at this stage in the preparation. Specific colors and color schemes may be needed, or it may be desirable to bring a random assortment of fabrics to a related tonal harmony. This is easily accomplished by dyeing the entire lot in a light wash of gray or in a pale wash of any color, either warm or cool in feeling, to coordinate evenly the color values of all the fabrics.

Strip cutting of fabric for hooking is best done with the straight of the goods. All knitted jerseys must be cut lengthwise, and not across from selvage to selvage, in order to prevent undue stretching and snapping back after hooking. Snip along the length of the woven fabric and tear it into strips in handy widths of 2″ or 3″, but not more than 6″. Tearing usually rips the fabric straight along the warp threads. Edges must be parallel to the straight of the warp before the cutting of the narrow hooking strips begins, or the strips will shred and pull apart. The final cut strip should retain the right angles of the weave. Do not sew the strips together to make longer lengths. Seams in the strips will jam the shuttle hookers and cannot be pulled through the backing fabric when they are hand-hooked.

STRIP CUTTING

There is no substitute for a sharp cutter. Shears should be long bladed, from 7″ to 8″ long. Use them for cutting fabric only, and have them reground when the blades grow dull, to keep them very sharp. A modestly effective home remedy for blunt scissors is to cut a piece of medium sandpaper again and again. Purists often prefer hand cutting to the use (and incidentally the expense) of cloth cutting machines. Some fuzzy or furry fabrics must be cut with a shears. However, busy craftsmen dedicated to rag hooked rugs will find that the machine cutter cuts uniformly, is extremely fast, may sometimes cut many strips at a time, and is infinitely kinder to the hands. There are free-standing models and others that must be clamped to the table. Some models take cutter wheels that are interchangeable, cutting from two to six strips at one time. The

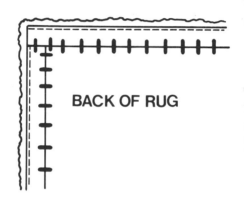

BACK OF RUG

Pulling the loops to the surface with the hand hook

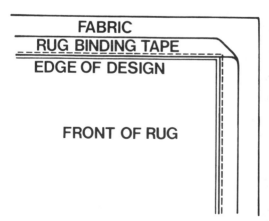

FABRIC
RUG BINDING TAPE
EDGE OF DESIGN

FRONT OF RUG

Binding a rug with tape. Above: The tape is applied before hooking begins. Top: Tape is turned to the back and hemmed after the rug is done.

sizes available are 3/32", cutting six strips at one time; 1/8", cutting four strips; 5/32" and 3/16", cutting three strips; and 1/4", cutting two strips. Another type that clamps to the table will take, in addition, a single strip cutter that can be adjusted to widths from 3/4" to 2" wide. This model is recommended because it can also be used for cutting strips for rug braiding. The manufacturers will exchange dull cutter wheels for new ones at a nominal cost. Precut sufficient strips in advance so as to avoid interruptions in work later. Store the strips according to color in clear plastic bags.

Because the types and weights of fabric will vary, the cloth strips may be cut in many different widths. As the foundation fabrics may differ, it is a good idea to make a test sample on a spare piece of the foundation fabric intended for use on a specific rug. Each test for width of cloth strip and the spacing between stitches and rows of stitches should be tried on a fair-sized sample—at least 3" square. Generally the width of the cloth strip will determine the height of the loop. The foundation fabric should not be visible when the test sample is viewed from above. The loops should appear even on the surface and close together without crowding each other.

THE SMALL HAND HOOK

When using a hand hooker of the crochet-needle type, grasp the hook around the wooden handle just above the steel shank. Hold it lightly, without tension, as you would a spoon or a pencil. The end of the hook is turned in the direction most suitable for lifting the cloth strip up through the foundation fabric. Usually the profile of the hook is held parallel to the body. However, the direction will change with curves and turns in the design, and when you have gained some experience, you will find it easier to maneuver without turning the frame. Hold the end of the cloth strip beneath the fabric with the other hand, with the long end of the strip between the index finger and the third finger, and the shorter end between the thumb and fourth finger. Push the hook through the surface of the fabric at an intersection between the warp and the weft. Pull up the end of the cloth strip to the front surface. Advance the hook and push it through the fabric one or two spaces away to grasp the cloth strip and pull it up to form a loop of the desired height. The thumb and index finger holding the cloth strip below the fabric will now be in a position to guide it around the hook. Borders and some designs look well when hooked in parallel rows, but flowers and curvilinear areas are more pleasing when the hooking follows the lines of the form. Even a large solid background of a single color benefits from a swirling pattern of hooking. When a color change is desired, or when the cloth strip reaches its end, pull the last part of the strip to the front surface of the foundation fabric. Start the next strip in the same space as the finished end. There will be two ends in one space.

(**Note:** All ends on rugs hooked by any method are drawn to the front surface. The reverse side of a hooked rug is flat and smooth. The ends mingling with the loops are later clipped to match the height of the loops. Strips are usually of varying lengths, staggering the endings. With all loops and ends firmly pulled up to the surface, it is unlikely that the nap will pull out.)

Outline the design elements in their own colors and then fill them in, or outline the background color around the design elements and then work the design areas. A combination of the two methods is probably the best. Working over the entire design areas rather than completing a segment at a time is helpful in judging color and maintaining an integrated color scheme.

Achieve a dimensional effect by changing the length of the loops. Gently curved areas are more practical than sudden height changes in rugs. Edges can be beveled by careful cutting with a raised-handle rug shears.

Lion, adapted from magazine instructions, by Dolores Wiemann. Hooked cloth strips with yarn loops

Hooked pillow cover by Jan Silberstein

On the Farm. Hooked rug. Collection Mr. and Mrs. Kenneth Maas

Alphabet rug by George Wells. Design adapted from a page in an early English spelling book. Punch-hooked with hand-dyed yarn

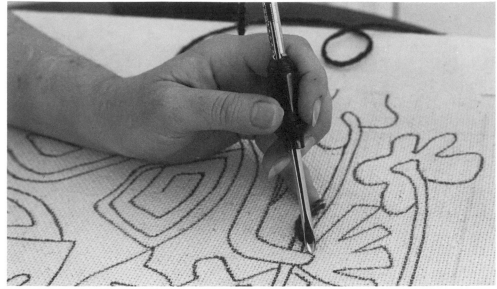

Threaded punch hook in position on a prepared design

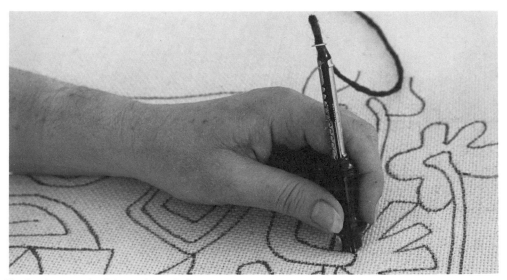

The hooker punched down through the canvas

PUNCH NEEDLES

The punch hook is one of a large group of contemporary hookers designed to speed up the process of rugmaking. It is not the fastest type, but it is undoubtedly more accurate because it is the most easily controlled. The foundation fabric, used in conjunction with any type of speed hooker, should be stretched taut on a frame. As the loops are pushed downward from the back of the fabric, the design as it appears drawn on the back of the fabric will emerge in reverse on the finished surface. Reverse the design before applying it to the fabric if it will describe the original concept more fully.

Although the punch needle may be worked with cloth strips, not every fabric is suitable, and the eye of the punch needle is limited in size. Use yarn of almost any kind that will draw through the needle freely. Wind all hanked yarn into balls. With the use of a swift, the hank of yarn wound around the swift can be fed directly into the punch needle from a strand that unwinds as the swift turns. Working directly from a swift is practical only when working large single-color areas or plain backgrounds. Having a large, flexible selection of yarn colors and textures ready and at hand is more important. Corrections and changes are easily made during hooking. Simply pull back on the last loop and keep pulling until as many loops as desired are released. Cut the yarn at the stopping point and push the cut end through to the front surface. A good

134

Punch needle and loops emerging on the opposite side

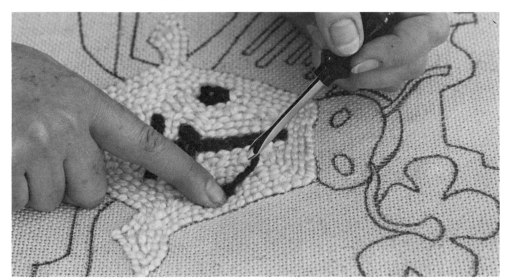

Withdrawing the needle before cutting thread

strong foundation fabric will withstand hooking more than once. Be careful when punching the needle through the fabric not to break or split the warp and the weft threads. If the holes appear too large, the warp and the weft can be pushed back into place with a blunt tapestry needle. The pressure of other areas of hooking near the corrected area will bring the warp and the weft back into position.

Become familiar with your punch needle. All types operate on the same basic principle. The yarn guide is a long, flat piece of metal folded up on both sides to form a central track designed to cup the yarn. The type of punch needle with a special hollow handle contains a locking device and a numbered series of ratchets for determining the length of the loop. The hollow-handled punch hook has interchangeable needles in two sizes. Insert the needle size suitable to the weight of the yarn or the number of strands to be used. Thread the yarn through the ring at the top of the handle and draw it loosely over the open track in the handle and the yarn needle. Push the yarn through the eye of the needle. Slide the yarn back and forth until it drops down into the track. The yarn must ride freely back and forth through the track. Allow about 1″ of yarn to protrude from the eye of the needle. The punch needle is held in the hand with the open track facing upward.

Be certain that the yarn will flow freely from the ball through the hooker

Rug designed by George Wells for a personal memento, a wife's gift to her husband. Hooked in yellow, blue, green, black, and pink. Courtesy Mr. and Mrs. John Colgate, Jr.

Gull by Dolores Wiemann. Hooked of narrow cloth strips. Form cut from background fabric, finished at the edges with Elmer's Glue-All, and mounted on a weathered plank

Phoenix Partially Consumed. Wall hanging hooked, brodded, and embroidered in hand-dyed yarn and sisal by the author

while you are working. Place a ball of yarn in a roomy box, a basket, or a bowl. If the ball of yarn is in a basket at your feet, it is helpful to draw the yarn up over your shoulder, pulling it down as needed. A single strand of heavy three-ply rug yarn or two strands of medium-weight yarn may be used in the larger needle. Two strands of yarn hooked in long loops can be cut to make a handsome shaggy appearance similar to that of a knotted rya rug. Space the rows about 1/2" apart. Fine yarns can be threaded three strands at a time through the larger needle. Punch hooks are relatively inexpensive and are pleasanter and more convenient to use when you are working with several colors. Two or three can be threaded with different combinations of yarn, eliminating the need for withdrawing the yarn and rethreading the hooker with each color change.

Punch the needle point down between the warp and the weft threads all the way to the hilt. With the other hand pull the cut end down underneath the foundation fabric to the right side. All cut ends must be pulled to the right side. Pull the needle up to the surface until only the point emerges. Do not pull the needle and yarn all the way out. When the point surfaces, ride it along the fabric for two threads and punch it down again. Keep the other hand on the surface of the fabric alongside the needle, pushing down slightly with the index finger as the needle is withdrawn. In order to stop hooking and cut the yarn, put the index finger over the last stitch and pull the needle up and back, exposing about 2" of yarn. Cut the yarn 1" from the end of the needle point. Push the remaining inch down to the right side with the point of the needle.

A taut surface is the key to even hooking. Check the right side every so often. Tug the loops down on the right side if there is any evidence of loose hooking on the side facing you. If necessary, tighten the foundation fabric on the frame. Start the second row at least a thread away from the previous row. Spacing between the rows is necessary to keep the rug flat and to allow room for the thickness of the yarn. Rows too close to each other crowd the stitches, causing irregularity and a slight puffing of the finished surface. On the other hand, loose packing will make the rug appear sparse and poorly constructed.

View from Above by Arni Frederiksen. Large hooked and painted wall hanging

Spanish Tile. Hooked rug designed by Joan Moshimer. Cloth strips in blues, golds, and rusts

HOOKING DIRECTION

Hooking should follow the forms of the design. Start with the outside edge of a curved area. Work around and around the contour, finishing at the center. Any composition with a central design on a solid background color can be worked in two parts. However, it is always best to keep the over-all color arrangement firmly in mind. Start by outlining the forms, then fill the interior areas. Using the background color, work around these forms, completing any small, irregular indentations that affect the central design. Then work the larger area of the background in one of several ways: Use vertical and horizontal rows, or a continuous hooking around and around the outside edge, finishing near the design; or consider introducing a curvilinear pattern, such as a scroll, a wave, or some other form in the single color of the background area. An all-over design is best hooked according to the contours of the design form, working in many different undulating curves. Interposing rigid vertical or horizontal rows into a design of this sort may cause a discordant pattern on the finished surface. Curving rows of hooking will move in a rhythmic mosaic pattern, blending the loops smoothly, without unusual interruptions.

Try not to cross over a finished row with the color from another row. Jumping produces a long stitch on the reverse side that could catch on something and cause the stitches to pull out. If you do jump rows, cut the long stitch on the reverse side in half and pull both cut ends through to the front surface. Trim the cut ends level with the pile. Check the front surface occasionally for sparse areas or uneven looping. Uneven looping can easily occur when the yarn fed into the punch hooker is impeded in any way. Sparse sections can be filled with supplementary rows, and uneven sections removed and rehooked. A single short loop, here and there, can be raised with a crochet hook. Work carefully, making certain that the short loop is not adjusted at the expense of the one next to it.

SHUTTLE HOOKING

The vigorous activity of shuttle hooking has a very special appeal for many people. By no means is it a quiet, gentle activity. It is as different from punch hooking as action painting is from miniature painting. The performance is somewhat similar to that of a dancer, a potter, or an athlete. The tool becomes an extension of oneself, demanding total involvement. A large, tightly stretched foundation fabric on a frame placed in an upright position presents the same challenge to the craftsman that the stretched canvas does to the painter. Although the large surface can be drawn and described in great detail for meticulous hooking, greater freedom is achieved by an interpretation from a smaller drawing. Observation and consideration of an entire working surface helps to suggest new images and solutions to design problems. The freedom to initiate the changes and to interweave new insights becomes essential, particularly as perception develops through experience with color and form. Vitality is one of the prime ingredients, and for some the principal factor in any work of art.

Shuttle hookers are designed in two parts, requiring both hands for operation; therefore the frame holding the foundation fabric must be self-supporting. A large frame can lean against a wall or be set in the open space provided by a door or window frame. A free-standing frame can be constructed with an easel base. Hinge the stand for the free-standing frame in sections so that it can be folded back for storage.

The basic principles in the operation of all types of shuttle hookers are similar. The adjustable needle point has two sections. One carries the yarn and as the yarn is pushed through the foundation fabric from the back, it

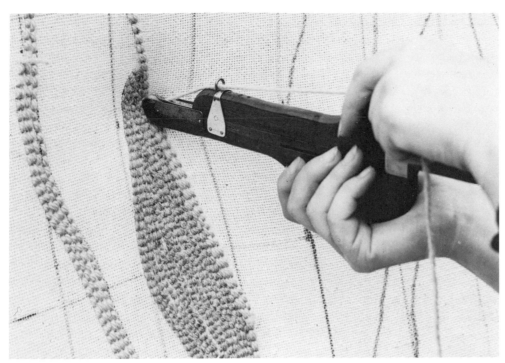

Speed shuttle in position for hooking

forms a loop. The other section of the needle then comes into play. From its raised position it slides down. A looper or a tongue riding inside the track in the needle holds the loop down and in place, permitting the needle to be withdrawn. The needle then automatically propels itself ahead to form the next loop. The needle point always leads, forming the loops first. Hold the shuttle hooker perpendicular to the foundation fabric. Both hands come into play as the sides of the needle move alternately. Establish an easy in-and-out rhythm. It is usual to hold the section containing the needle in the more agile hand. However, it is extremely important to become accustomed to working up and down, to the left and to the right with facility. Follow the manufacturer's directions for threading the needle. As always with hooking, the spacing between rows depends upon the weight of the yarn and the depth of the pile. Longer loops can easily be spaced about 1/8" or a bit farther apart. Space shorter loops closer together. The test of correct spacing is in whether or not the foundation fabric is visible on the right side. If the fabric is visible, the rows are too widely spaced. However, do not crowd the rows of stitches. Hook the outline of the form first. Turn a corner or change direction with the flat tongue looper in the down position. Do not remove the hooker except to cut the yarn. Place the index finger on the last stitch and pull the shuttle hooker back about two inches, cutting the yarn in the center without unthreading the needle. Push the cut end of the yarn through to the right side with the point of the needle.

Depth of pile is a matter of choice. Unclipped rugs usually have a nap that varies from 1/4" to 1/2". If the rug is to be clipped, the loops should be deeper, to allow for inserting scissors. Vary the length of the loops for a change in texture or to effect a raised relief. Odd lengths of yarn emerging here and there on the front surface for special effects can be made by pulling the yarn from the eye of the needle while it is in the down position underneath the foundation fabric.

Speed hookers require a steady source of free-flowing yarn. If the loops are uneven or the hooking stops, check the ball of yarn. Knots in the yarn must be cut away and the hooker rethreaded. The backing fabric must always retain its tautness. Tighten the fabric as soon as any slack is noticeable.

Hooking a large canvas stretched on a frame loom

CLIPPING HOOKED RUGS

Rag rugs will wear better if left unclipped. Yarn rugs wear equally well whether clipped or looped. The loops of a short napped rug should be split open with small, sharp, long-bladed scissors, but it is possible to cut off the tops of longer loops by using special rug shears with a raised handle. It is advisable to clip the tops of rugs as the work progresses in order to insure an even pile. Insert the blade of the scissors into several loops at a time, pulling the blade up high before cutting. If the pile is clipped after the whole rug has been completed, cut the loops open and then trim with a rug shears to even the pile. A textured wall hanging can be trimmed at any time. Sometimes it is helpful to hang the piece on the wall and take time to study the possible finished effect before cutting. Consider and plan the areas to be trimmed or fluffed. After cutting, a fluffier effect can be achieved by rubbing the strands of yarn between the fingers, opening the plied yarn. There are many possibilities. A pile can be sheared for a velvety appearance, or remain looped, or the pile can be sheared and looped in combination. The height of a rug can be uniform or the pile can be cut in varying depths. The shearing of the yarn reveals a slight change in the appearance of the color. A deeper, more intense color is apparent after cutting.

FINISHING HOOKED RUGS

Spreading the back of the rug with a latex finish stabilizes the hooked stitches, locking them in position. Latexing also adds body to the rug and retards skidding. Remove the rug from the frame when it is completely finished and all corrections have been made. As it is necessary to stretch the rug looped side down for latexing, select a large, flat surface suitable for stapling, such as plywood or some type of pressed board. Outline the original size on the board, using a colored pencil or a felt-tipped pen and ruler. Fit the rug, face down, to the ruled line. Place several staples (thumbtacks or carpet tacks can also be used) along one edge of the hem to hold the rug in place. Staple or tack the center of the opposite side and the left and right sides. Gradually tack all around the edges of the rug, pulling it to fit the guideline. Of course, if the frame is large enough to hold the full rug, the back can be latexed without removing it from the frame. Latex can be purchased in department or hard-

Rug shears with raised handle for level clipping

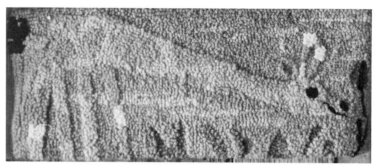

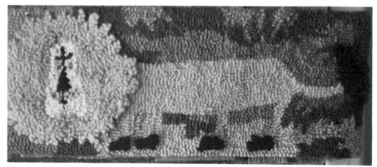

Rug by Lola Sherwin hooked with green, red, white, black, and brown wool

Above: *Cow, Giraffe, Hippo,* and *Lion.* Four hooked wool stair treads by the author

Black-and-white-design hooked rug by Virginia Pedulla, based on Spanish black work

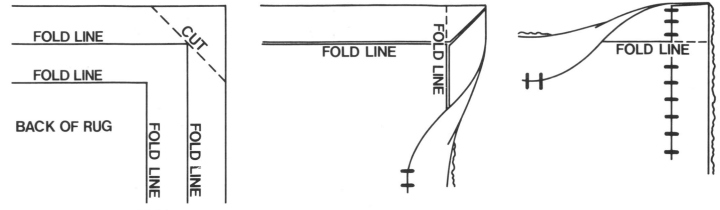

Steps in making a squared finish

ware stores, or from firms specializing in rugmaking supplies. This very sticky substance is also available in self-dispensing plastic bags and bottles. One quart generally covers from nine to twelve square feet of rug, depending upon the thickness of the composition of the latex. Work in a well-ventilated room. Apply the latex in an organized fashion, a section at a time, spreading it evenly with a wide spatula made of cardboard or with a putty knife. Thin latex may be painted on with a paintbrush, but cleaning the brush may be a concern. Latex is waterproof; therefore clean the brush immediately with detergent in warm water. If the latex is accidentally spilled on clothing, wash it off as soon as possible. Do not spread the latex beyond the hooked area as it will make hemming difficult. Let the rug dry thoroughly. Drying may take eight hours or more, depending upon the size of the rug and the density of the latex. It is not necessary to use latex on the back of wall hangings, although the firmer surface provided by a backing of thin latex may be desirable.

HEMMING

Remove the staples carefully and place the rug on the floor if it is very large. Smaller pieces can be hemmed more comfortably on a table. About 2″ of fabric is satisfactory for a hem. Draw a line around the rug 2″ away from the looped edge. Trim any excess fabric. There are two ways to turn and fold the corners:

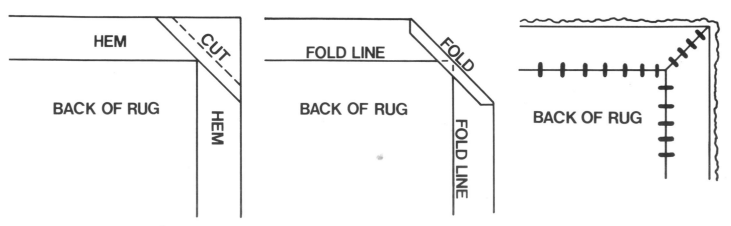

Steps in making a mitered finish

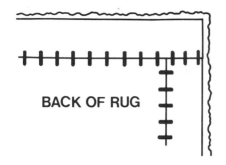

BACK OF RUG

Reverse side of a hooked rug, showing hem

1 Miter the corners of square or rectangular rugs, to trim the excess fabric for a flat appearance without lumpiness. Turn the point at the corner of the hem down to meet the corner of the rug. Cut this triangular section away. Turn the corner section down again. Fold the sides to the left and right of the corner in half and then fold down again, bringing the two sides together evenly. Pin in place. Complete all sides, pinning them before hemming.

2 Trim the corners by folding the points of the fabric in to meet the corners of the rug. Cut away the triangular section. (A bit more could be trimmed off the corners, but never cut too near the looping as any fraying could impair the foundation fabric.) Fold the hem almost halfway in toward the looping, stopping about ⅛" away from the loops. Fold the adjacent side. Holding the area near the corner down with the fingers, turn one side straight down and the adjacent side straight over it. The corner will be square and flush with the edge of the rug. Pin the fabric in place and complete the other corners. Fold and pin along the sides.

Hem all edges with heavy linen or cotton carpet thread. There are adhesives composed of thick latex that will paste the hem to the rug backing. These edge binders (which come in plastic bags) are easy to apply by following the manufacturer's instructions. Latex edge binders will seal any cut edges in danger of fraying. Apply over the diagonal mitered opening. Elmer's Glue-All or Sobo Glue, white sticky milk products that are colorless after application, will also seal edges easily.

Finishing. Mitered corners ready for turning

Binding pinned in place, ready for hemming

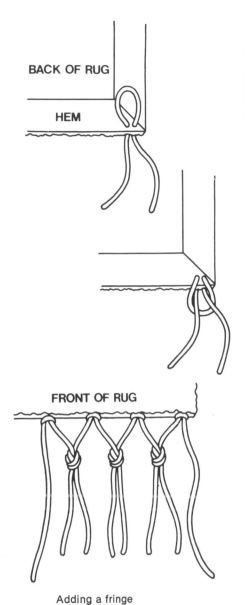

BACK OF RUG

HEM

FRONT OF RUG

Adding a fringe

Three Graces by the author. Hooked in black and white yarn with embroidery and photographs

View from Within by Arni Frederiksen. Detail of large wall hanging with a hooked, painted, and collage surface

144

HEMMING A ROUND RUG

With the aid of a ruler, mark off the area of the hem by placing a series of dots two inches away from the edge of the looping, at close intervals all around the circular rug. Connect the dots, using a felt-tipped marker, and mark a double set of lines 1″ apart. Draw a line on the back of the foundation fabric, across the diameter of the circle, with a felt-tipped pen. The exact center of the circle can be found by folding the circle in half. Fold again in the opposite direction and draw another line through the center, forming a cross. Using these as guidelines, mark lines radiating out from the center hem about two inches apart and evenly spaced along the perimeter.

With scissors cut along these lines from the outside, stopping 1/8″ away from the loops. Do not cut into the loops. Carefully fold each cut section halfway in and then fold again. Pin each section to the foundation fabric consecutively, overlapping each one in succession. Work around the circle, overlapping each section in the same direction. Hem with carpet thread or latex paste. Use latex to seal the cut edges.

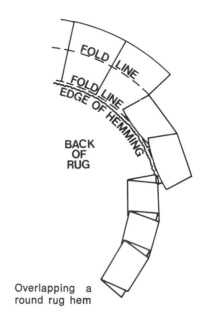

Overlapping a round rug hem

Burning Bush by the author. Rug of hand-dyed multicolored yarns

Felt appliqué wall hanging, padded and top-stitched on the sewing machine, a design inspired by nature and adaptable to many techniques

146

Eagle. A small rug by Mr. and Mrs. Joseph Dobbs, based on a Navajo design. Photo by the author

NATURE PLAYS AN IMPORTANT ROLE in the shaping of our lives. We are of it, part of it, one with it every moment. Opening our eyes on a new day, another day, is the wonder of all days. Contemplate the rain, feel the sun shining, speculate on the threatening atmosphere. Is the air heavy, the breeze soft, the water warm, the water too cold; is the blue reflecting the sky or does the grayness portend change? Visual impressions, emotional reactions, and intuitive feelings immediately flood consciousness in a steady flow of thought, all considerable subject matter for designing. Think of designing as a method of recording or conveying ideas in the same manner one would describe them in a diary, or discuss them across the breakfast table over coffee. A good story is told in simplified form to make the point stronger. All details are sifted, and the most striking chosen for effective support. After all, the instant of reality is past, the retelling must be a visual illusion, a sharing of experiences through a series of impressions. Design in art is a universal mark of humanity, as is the written and spoken word in language.

It is a mistake to confuse all impressions of form with the expression of the European painters of the Renaissance. Everyone is familiar with the Renaissance concern for rendering deep space through the use of minute color changes from light to dark, in the interests of depicting reality. The lovely Unicorn tapestries of the sixteenth century, woven by Flemish weavers to commemorate a royal marriage, were an early attempt at creating an appearance of rounded forms by gradually tinting and toning the colors of the weft yarns. Since the predawn of history, the weavers of the rest of the world, from continent to continent, from the Indians of the Americas to the nomads of the

DESIGN

Silk Afghanistan hunting rug. Detail. Collection Norma Kershaw

147

Caucasus, had executed design elements on a broader scale and from an entirely different point of view. Although they may be intricately detailed, they are never conceived of as an imitation of life. Whatever the conditions, art is always a reaffirmation of all that is good in human life. Perhaps the Navajo philosophy expressed in this translation of the weaver's poem will provide a deeper understanding of the symbolism of their designs:

> May the warp be the white light of morning,
> May the weft be the red light of evening,
> May the fringes be the falling rain,
> May the border be the standing rainbow.
>
> Thus weave for us a garment of brightness
> That we may walk fittingly where birds sing,
> That we may walk fittingly where grass is green,
> Oh our Mother the Earth, oh our Father the Sky.
> —from *Songs of the Tewa* by Herbert J. Spinden

Most designs of any stylistic development must be guided by the technique used. Detailed designs of horsemen galloping across a pile carpet of silken fibers from Afghanistan may require from 300 to 500 knots per square inch to represent the slenderness of the horses' speeding legs, the variations and refinement of figures in magnificent raiment. On the other hand, the Scandinavian rya rug may have no more than 8 to 16 knots per square inch, and still describe the feeling of movement differently but just as effectively. The number of knots determines the time spent making the carpet rather than the size of the carpet. The enormous flat-woven tapestry weaves of the seventeenth century may have as many as 50 or more weft threads per inch, tightly beaten down on a warp count of 18 threads to the inch. The Navajo blankets vary according to the spinning and their date of production. Blankets woven before 1865 may have from 20 to 40 weft threads per inch, but more contemporary ones vary widely with counts as low as 8 weft threads to the inch.

Diamond and *Four Trees,* two rugs by Mr. and Mrs. Joseph Dobbs, based on Navajo designs

Stained-glass window in the home of Mr. and Mrs. George Wiemann

Rug by Dolores Wiemann inspired by the window at left

Galaxy by Vesta B. Ward. Appliquéd padded felt on linen background

Naturally, the count of the warp and weft, in addition to determining speed of execution, influences the degree of the staggered steps necessary to outline a form. The lower the warp and the weft count the less complexity and detail possible in the design.

Other techniques are controlled by the type of tool used. In the same way that a fine pen point is capable of making fine lines, so the finer hooking needle, crochet hook, or knitting needle, when coupled with finer yarn, will produce more and narrower stitches per inch than a heavy one. Simplify the design and limit complicated detail when working in broad techniques on modest-size pieces.

Good design lies in the organization of the elements necessary to the composition of art. A great design comes from someplace deep within, where the records of our own concerns and interests are kept. The basic elements of design, form, color, line, texture, and an awareness of three-dimensional space are only equipment that enables the artist to express his needs freely. When the work breathes with the quality of our personal lives and relationships and the authority of our own experiences, a presence is formed that is recognized as the creativity of the artist.

A rug can be called a wall hanging, but not all wall hangings have the prerequisites of a rug. Obviously, a rug must be sturdy, somewhat practical, skidproof, and in almost all cases should complement a given interior. Wall hangings today are purely decorative, and in some interiors they become an important focal point.

Color and the texture inherent in the technique are the dominant design considerations in most rugs. Others, such as hearth rugs or those chosen specifically as works of art, incorporate all of the elements of design.

COLOR

Perhaps color is the single most complex element in design, visually and emotionally. Color stimulates or soothes, alerts as a symbol of danger, or signals that all is well. It can be warm or cool or pleasantly neutral. Individuals have both intuitive and personal reactions to color. A small child may well feel that happiness is a red lollipop.

149

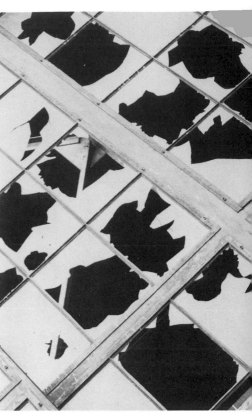

Rug of cut and uncut multicolored felt strips machine sewn ½″ apart to a burlap backing fabric. The overlapping strips were trimmed after completion in wide, shallow, undulating curves—another way to make shaggy, colorful rugs

In the City Windows, a photograph by Alan Sweetman

Color is apparent only in the presence of light. In the absence of light everything appears to be black. The eye cannot separate an object from its background without some color contrast. The glory of Scandinavian ryas is the subtle game the artist-craftsman plays with color values. Many different colors are employed in close values of varying intensities, maintaining a barely discernible form. Hue, value, and intensity are the three dimensions of color. Hue is the pure state of the three primary colors—red, yellow, and blue. Each primary color when combined with another primary color produces the secondary colors—orange, green, and violet, all clear hues. Further combinations of the primary colors with the secondary colors are known as the tertiary colors, again clear hues. Value can refer to the colors as they range from light to dark. Yellow is the lightest and blue violet the darkest. However, the reference is usually to the tints and tones of each color. Differences in intensity produce the greatest subtlety in color. Changes occur in the intensity of the pure form of the hue when the purity is dulled by introducing small amounts of the color on the opposite side of the color wheel. Colors opposite each other on the color wheel are known as complementary colors, and when the proportion mixed becomes equal, they produce a neutral brownish color.

Have you ever noticed how all natural fibers go well together? Never are the sheep out of harmony with the fields while grazing. Vegetable dyeing for color is always successful but requires a great deal of preparation and accessible resources. The secret of bringing commercially prepared yarns into harmony with each other lies in overdyeing the yarn. (Most commercially dyed colors benefit from a light redyeing in a watered wash of the complementary color.) Use the prepared packets of dye, wetting the yarn thoroughly before immersion in the dye bath. If you have purchased yarn in primary colors, prepare your own secondary and tertiary colors for subtle, unusual results. For in-

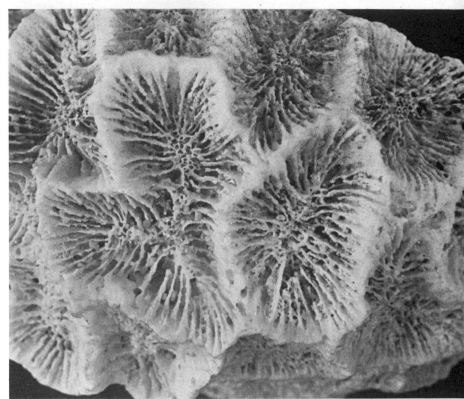

The Sea. An artist's interpretation, by Peter Marein

Coral

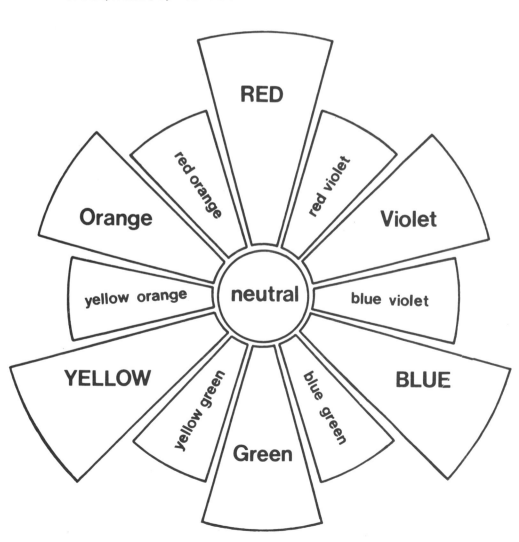

stance, experiment with yellow yarn by trying a light wash of orange dye for a yellow orange, or a thin wash of red for a red orange. After drying, a second thin wash of a complementary color will gray the color. A light wash of green will turn yellow orange to an olive color. Always make test swatches before dyeing large quantities. Keep records of the relative amounts of dye to water and of other color variations by tagging the dry swatch with the dyeing information. Sectional dyeing varies the color within one skein. Pull sections of the

The hibiscus as inspiration for a design can be approached from many points of view. Not every interpretation is suited to every medium. Intricate detail is possible in embroidery and needlepoint, but pile rugs should be broad in concept. Still, the same subject can be adapted to each medium.

Silhouette the pertinent subject matter from its background, particularly if the complexity of material is great. Use a well-sharpened pencil or pen and ink. Select suitable material from the background and adapt it to the basic shape of the design area. Try different arrangements on tracing paper, overlaying and repeating sections by reversing the tracing paper. Indicate color with Magic Markers or colored pencils. Numbers can do so, or symbols can be used instead to indicate the various colors.

The design in needlepoint

yarn out of the dye bath, resting it over the side of the pot while the portion remaining in the pot deepens in color due to its prolonged immersion in the simmering water. Remember to dye the yarn in skeins tied in at least three places with loosely knotted cord to prevent tangling. Balls of yarn can be dyed too, but the interior will be much lighter than the exterior and the yarn will require a longer drying time. Follow the directions for dyeing given on the packet.

For a broader interpretation select and enlarge an interesting section of the design. A simple way to crop a design is to move a small cutout paper frame over the surface until you find the most satisfying part.

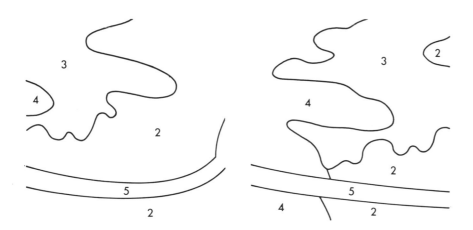

Further enlargement maintains the essence of the original, but with greater subtlety. Enlarge the sketch again for an abstract appearance and perhaps the emergence of an entirely new form.

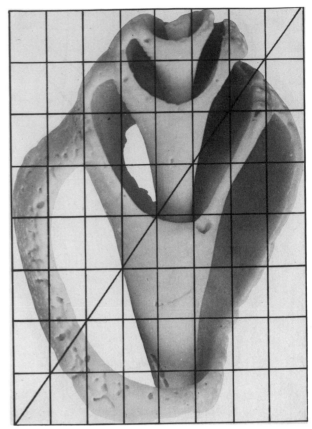

Drawing the shell to scale

Sensitivity is the capacity to observe objects appreciatively, in the home, at work, or on vacation. Train your eye to speculate on the structure of forms and to enjoy the relationship of one part to another. Study an object up close and from a distance, by feeling it, by squinting at it with veiled eyes. Observe it from every viewpoint with patience. Take it out of its original context, studying it in a new relationship to get the clearest and most satisfactory impression. Here we must illustrate with photographs, but there is no substitute for the fullness of reality. The photograph is helpful as reference material.

Enlarge or reduce a sketch for transferring the design or for the purpose of breaking up the design into smaller, proportional areas. Although a design cannot be transferred precisely to a warp, finding a halfway point or other sectional division is a helpful guide to transferring proportions. Rug hookers also find a color sketch divided with a grid convenient. Work directly on the surface of the sketch, dividing it into squares. If the original must be preserved intact, tape a large piece of tracing paper or acetate over the surface. Enclose or box the design area. If only a single form is to be enlarged, closely surround that form. If a border area is desired, include it in the grid. Draw a diagonal line from left to right, from the lower left-hand corner to the upper right-hand corner and beyond it. To enlarge the form, draw a new horizontal and vertical from a point on the diagonal line that reaches beyond the upper right-hand corner. Reduce the form by choosing any point on the diagonal line that is within the original form and drawing a new horizontal and vertical line within the form. Divide the original piece of artwork into halves, into quarters, into sixteenths. Draw the enlarged or reduced size directly on the fabric or on another piece of paper and divide it into the same number of squares as the original. Transfer outlines of the images from box to box.

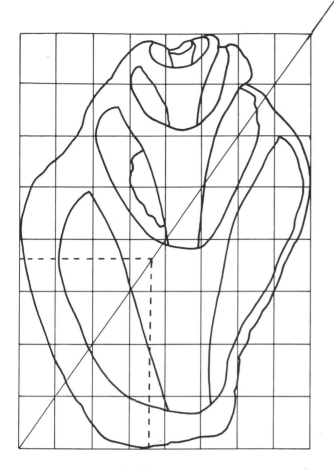

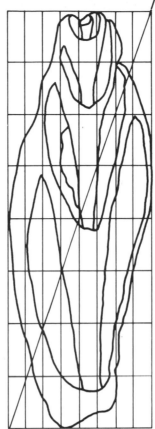

Exaggerating the form by changing the proportions of the divisions

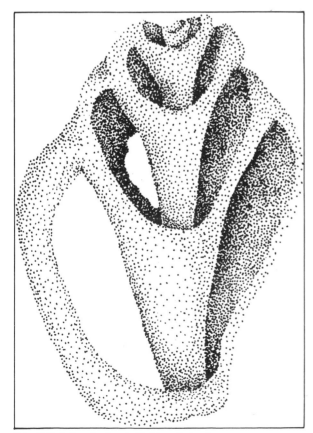

Rendering the design in light and shade

Outlining the areas strongly

155

Outlining the areas with thick and thin lines

Reversing the image

Solar coral

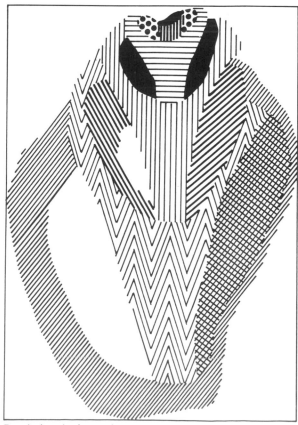

Rendering the image in areas of texture

156

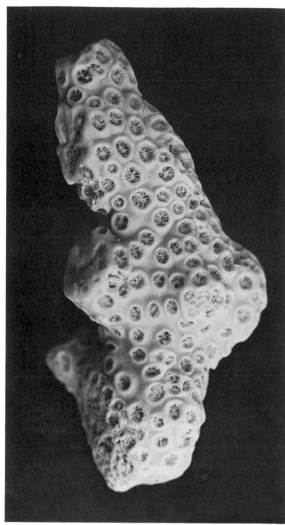

Coral craters

Brain coral form

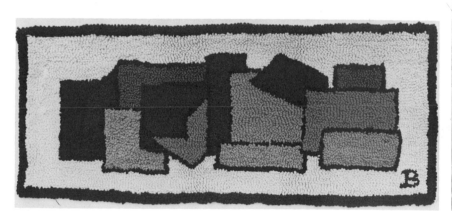

Hooked rug by Barbara Barron based on an arrangement of pieces of paper

Patterns formed by cross sections of logs

157

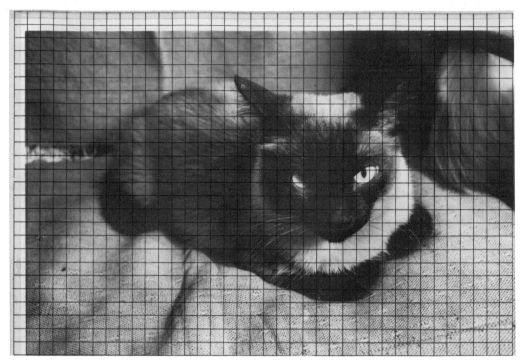

Interpretation of a photographic image according to values from light to dark. Place a half-inch grid across the surface of the subject, on tracing paper or acetate. Baccus. *Photo Mary Velthoven*

Simplify the changes in value by determining how few or how many changes are necessary to delineate the form. On this design the transitional areas were limited to five color changes. Shade the areas, using solids, lines, and crosshatching Select the tints and tones of the colors according to the value of the shaded areas.

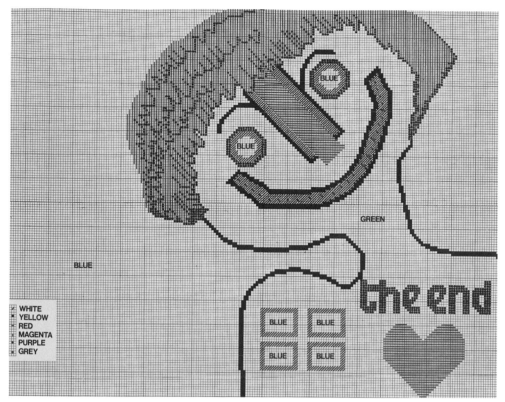

WHITE
YELLOW
RED
MAGENTA
PURPLE
GREY

BLUE

GREEN

BLUE

the end

BLUE   BLUE

BLUE   BLUE

Design for the hooked rug below, graphed to indicate color placement

the end

Lay Me Out with a Smile by the author. Cross-stitch and latchet hooking on canvas

Variations on a rectangle divided horizontally

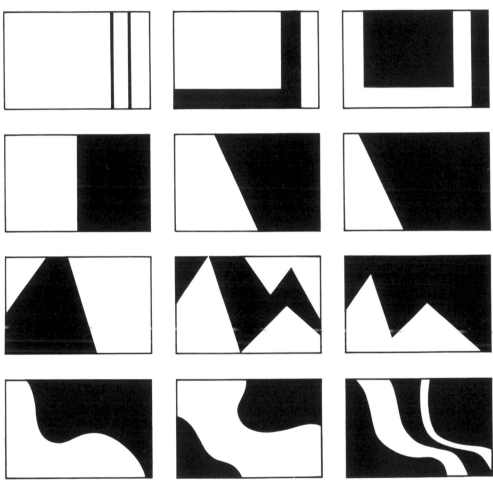

Twelve compositions within a rectangle

FORM AND LINE

Form and line are similar, or at least closely related, in that a line will enclose a space, delineating a form. Every rug or wall hanging will have a basic form or shape within the limitations of the medium used. It has been noted by many householders that the square form is the least adaptable to interior space. Loom-constructed fabrics are limited to some extent by the size of the loom; all designing takes place within a set perimeter. The treatment of relationships within a rectangle is limitless. Make test doodles on a series of identical shapes, breaking the composition horizontally in as many ways as possible. Shade one half to stress the division in light and dark tones. The simple procedure of breaking a rectangular composition horizontally will bring to mind a landscape. Make additional compositions based on vertical divisions to evoke a forest of tree trunks. Try curvilinear forms. Enlarge the compositions with cutout pieces of colored paper. Think about the arrangement, moving the pieces around until the elements are satisfactory, before pasting them down.

Design after a Joan Miró painting, hooked by Marsha Wolff

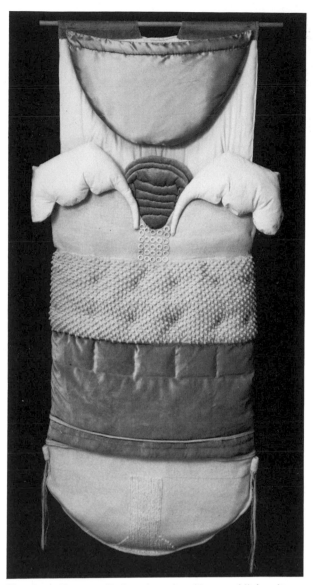

Sleeping Bag, wall hanging by Norma Minkowitz. Knitted, crocheted, and padded construction of muslin, velvet, and satin. Photo Little Bobby Hanson

At this point it is a good idea to set the designs aside, returning to them at a later time with objectivity. Magic Marker or cut paper additions may be necessary. The composition is workable if after repeated consideration it appears to fulfill aesthetically the function it is designed to serve.

Little innovation has occurred in rugmaking since the creative breakthrough of the shaggy, freely woven Scandinavian rya technique. Power-driven broadlooms have provided decades of wall-to-wall carpeting, satisfying almost everyone's need for status, for warmth, and for beautiful fields of color and texture. Surfeit to the point of saturation is an understatement when one realizes that astrodomes as well as bathrooms are carpeted with broadloom. The reaction of the iconoclast is to search for choicer morsels. Bare floors are again providing polished backgrounds for uniquely individual handmade rugs, as well as for priceless pile Orientals and flat-woven kilims. Another interesting development is the introduction of handmade pile and hooked rugs as wall hangings in limited editions. Designs for these editions are selected from the work of esteemed contemporary European and American artists sponsored by leading art galleries.

Victorian cross-stitch rug, c. 1850. Collection Edward Jamgotchian

Hedgerow by Maggi Jo Norton. Detail. Embroidered hanging inspired by a thorn hedge in full flower. Collection Sidlaw Industries, Dundee, Scotland

EM-BROIDERED RUGS AND WALL HANGINGS

Peruvian textile border fragment in Tiahuanaco style. Collection of the author

FEW PEOPLE ARE AWARE that many rugs are embroidered rather than hooked or woven. Any surface treatment performed with a threaded sewing needle is essentially a stitchery technique. Many handmade rya rugs from Scandinavia (other than those woven on hand or power looms) are embroidered. The rya knot, which is the same as the Ghiordes knot used in Turkish rugs but quite a bit longer, can be worked with a needle on a prepared foundation fabric. As an embroidery stitch, the knot is called turkey work. Of English origin, the term "turkey work" was an early description of all Eastern pile rugs.

During the Tudor period embroidery on both fabric and canvas flourished in England as a popular pastime. Chair seats and footstools were covered in embroidered turkey work imitating Oriental pile rugs. Knotted turkey work was well established as an embroidery technique by the end of the seventeenth century.

Embroidery always presupposes a foundation fabric to hold the decorative surface stitches. Canvas is an ancient material, originally made from hemp. In needlework, canvas is a term loosely applied to any type of fiber woven openly enough so that the needle can be easily inserted between the warp and the weft without splitting the fibers. There is evidence that the Romans embroidered on an open mesh fabric very similar to canvas. The pre-Columbian Peruvians used both agave fibers and heavy cotton in natural brown and white for foundation fabric. Most canvas today is made of cotton or linen, often sized to provide stiffness.

Satin stitch, stem stitch, and chain stitch are some of the universally known stitches that have been in continuous use for the embroideries of civilizations as widely separated as those of ancient China and Peru. Of course, not all embroidery stitches are suitable or practical for rugmaking. Long stitches with little attachment to the backing fabric have a tendency to pull and stretch after prolonged use. Most stitches placed close together and worked with sturdy rug yarn will produce long-lasting, flat-surfaced rugs. Chain stitch in its many versions will cover the largest amount of surface area, leaving only the most economical amount of yarn on the reverse side.

Texture can be introduced to the flat surface by using raised stitches. For instance, the simple cross stitch gains prominence when the ordinary X cross stitch is worked first and then overlaid with an upright cross stitch. If you use a variety of stitches in your design, try to do so judiciously, to avoid the experimental look of an unintentional sampler. Of course, a planned patchwork sampler of various stitches can also be an attractive design. Pile areas, of either turkey work or latchet hooking, set off specific design areas and combine well with embroidery stitches. Embroidery stitches and needlepoint stitches are interchangeable. Most embroidery stitches are easily adapted to needlepoint canvas, so do not be afraid to experiment with them on rug canvases. Needlepoint embroiderers are patient, tireless, and prolific craftsmen, often working endlessly on pillow tops. They might profit from the example of their Victorian ancestors who produced good-sized carpets by assembling individual needlepoint squares. Cross stitch was most frequently used in Victorian days because it is more durable than tent stitch. The largest carpet of this period was made for Queen Victoria and measured 29′ x 30′. The design was planned and painted as a complete picture on a type of graph paper, then cut up and worked in 150 squares, each about 2′ square. The design was composed of geometric and floral motifs connected by wreaths of leaves and decorative foliage.

FOUNDATION MATERIALS

Monk's cloth and Duraback are both very satisfactory background fabrics for embroidered rugs and wall hangings. They are very strong, and the intersections of the warp and the weft are clearly visible and easily counted. For a turkey work pile withdraw and remove every eighth weft thread. Withdrawing threads serves as a guideline to help maintain even rows of knotting and also allows room for the formation of the knots, particularly when several strands of yarn are used at one time. Equal spacing of about ½″ between rows of knots allows for the settling of the pile. Monk's cloth and Duraback are available in many widths up to 16′. Burlap and jute fabrics make reasonably strong backings and are more modestly priced. Less durable backings will last for many years, depending upon the traffic and the abrasiveness of the surface upon which they are placed. Dampness is probably the single factor most detrimental to rug backings, so consider where the rug will be used.

A beautifully prepared backing for rya knotting is available from Scandinavia. About six rows of woolen plain weave alternate with an unwoven space left for adding embroidered knots. This sturdy foundation fabric is firmly woven on a linen warp and completely finished except for the insertion of the rya knots. The spacing between knotting rows is about ⅝″, so long, shaggy rya knots are needed for coverage.

Handsome upholstery fabric will provide a good background for wall hangings. Some areas of the fabric can be left exposed, and others embroidered with flat or pile surfaces. Small pieces, such as narrow widths of drapery fabric, can be assembled alternately with sections of Duraback.

Also available and very easy to work with is a double-mesh rug canvas backing made especially for rya knots. It has very large square mesh spaces between rows of ⅜″ twisted plain weave. Filling the spaces requires very thick yarn, or four or five single strands used together. Regular double-weave rug canvas of the same type as the kind used for latchet hooking is also suitable. This type of canvas makes possible tight rows of knots without any plain-weave spacing between rows. Short knots will produce an upright pile of loops if left uncut, or they can be cut to make a velvety surface. Another effect can be achieved by alternating, on every row, the warp threads around which the knots are tied.

Double-woven canvas, particularly canvas with a twist in the warp threads and five mesh spaces per inch, is recommended for needlepoint rugs. Three- and four-mesh-spaced canvas is available but requires heavier yarn to cover the canvas backing.

Choose a backing that is suitable to the technique, the purpose, and the width of the work. If small pieces are joined, overlap them 2″ and work through the double thickness. Estimate the amount of fabric yardage, including an extra 2″ all around for hemming. Canvas mesh backings require only 1″ all around for turning under or hemming. Selvages on canvas backing must be taken into consideration. Many people work right up to the selvage, but the rug will wear better if the amount turned under is evenly balanced all around. The hem can be incorporated in the embroidery by turning under the last three or four mesh spaces, lining them up, and stitching through them as a unit. Prevent raw edges from fraying by binding them with masking tape while working. The edges of fabric foundations can be safeguarded with tape, overcasting, or a long running stitch on the sewing machine. Rug binding can be machine-sewn to the fabric foundation before working to make a finished edge ready for hemming without overcasting. Irregular shapes on square or rectangular foundations should not be cut out until the work is completed.

Remember to allow for the hem when positioning the design for transfer. Define and clearly mark the outside limits of the rug shape on the foundation fabric with a felt-tipped pen, then outline the interior design areas. Colored markers make the design easy to follow.

There is no need to stretch the fabric on hoops or a frame for knotted turkey work, but some embroidery stitches done on a soft foundation are more successfully worked on a stretcher.

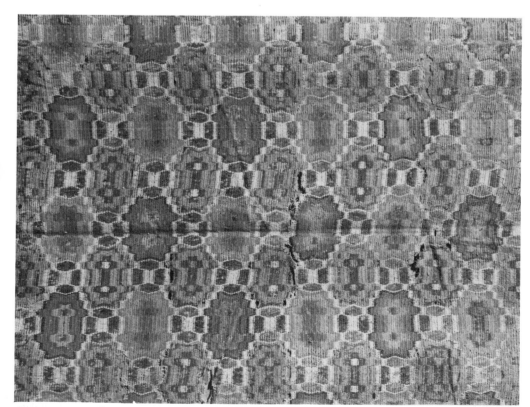

Portuguese needlepoint rug, sixteenth century. Collection Edward Jamgotchian

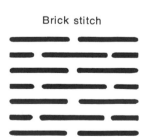

Brick stitch

Asian tent hanging embroidered in a daisy pattern. Collection Michael Silbert

Turkey work on burlap by Linda Lippe. Rug made by a high-school student, using a design based on an arrangement of the letters of her name

YARNS

More and more yarns today are synthetics or blended compositions. These yarns are excellent for rugs because they are inelastic, resist moths, and generally wear well. However, they do seem to lack the soft, buttery quality we have come to expect of fine wools. It is always sensible to purchase yarns of the best quality available within one's budget. Yarns can be purchased in bulk at home and abroad from suppliers specializing in yarn for carpet mills and home weavers. Shopping is advised, and samples, if available, should be requested. Rug yarns come in heavy, medium, and light weights. Most short-pile rugs are of one type of yarn, but shag rugs are often more interesting from the point of view of color and texture if the different weights are mixed. If possible, try to avoid using knitting worsted, but leftover bits can be used in small amounts when combined with other, stronger yarns.

Turkey-work rugs made on a prepared foundation with a plain-weave spacing of about ½", with loops about 1½" long, spaced approximately 11 or 12 knots every three inches, will require about 8½ ounces of yarn per square foot. A 2′ × 3′ rug therefore will use about 3½ pounds of yarn. Cost can be determined in advance by making a 1′ square sample practice piece using scraps of yarn similar to that which you intend to buy and weighing the sample, deduct-

Angel Cosmique by Aurelia Muñoz.
Split-stitch embroidery

Rug in a stained-glass design done
on Scandinavian backing by Gunnel
Teitel

ing the weight of the canvas. If you have one, use a balancing baby scale of
the kind that measures ounces with small weights. In the absence of a home
scale, use the consumers' weight-check scale at the supermarket. Multiply the
weight of the square foot by the square footage of the planned rug. Square
footage is determined by multiplying the width by the length of the rug. For
instance, a rug measuring 5' × 7' equals a 35' square area. When the materials
include yarns of mixed weights, figure the proportion of each type. A very
shaggy 5' × 7' rug with knots 2" or 3" long might have four single strands in
each knot composed of one lightweight, two medium-weight, and one heavyweight yarn. Depending upon the type of yarn, a total of about 22 pounds
might be needed; therefore you will want half the total poundage in medium-
weight yarn, approximately one-third of the remainder in lightweight yarn, and
the remaining two-thirds in heavyweight yarn.

Once the approximate amount of poundage, and a bit over, is determined for
the total square footage of the rug, you will be able to estimate the amount of
each color from your color sketch. For instance, if two thirds of the rug is red
and one third is white, divide these amounts into the total weight in order to
determine how many pounds of each to purchase.

NEEDLES

Yarn needles are blunt and thick, with long, wide eyes that will easily hold four or five single yarns of different weights. Threading these needles is relatively simple. Pinch the end of the yarn between index finger and thumb and push it through the wide eye. If several strands of yarn are used together, be sure the end of each strand is level with the next one before pushing them through the eye. If they are irregular, cut the grouping straight across.

GLOSSARY

YARN NEEDLE

Heavy, blunt, long, wide-eyed needle for yarn.

TURKEY WORK, CUT

A basic knotted embroidery stitch, cut to produce a velvet pile.

TURKEY WORK, UNCUT

The uncut, knotted embroidery stitch with looped pile.

CHAIN STITCH

Circular loops linked together to cover large surface areas.

CROSS STITCH

A durable stitch practical for embroidered or needlepoint rugs.

RUG CANVAS

A three- to five-mesh canvas suitable for embroidered rugs.

RYA KNOT CANVAS

A three-mesh canvas with plain weave spaced between the rows of mesh.

STITCHES

There are hundreds of embroidery and needlepoint stitches. A great many are handsome additions to wall hangings, but not all are suited to large-scale hangings, and some are too time-consuming and impractical for rugs. The straight stitch, half cross stitch, cross stitch, chain stitch, and knotted stitches are basic constructions with many variations. The continental and basket-weave versions of the half cross stitch are firmer needlepoint stitches, but because they require more yarn on the reverse side, cross stitch, with its double-fronted surface, has much to recommend it. However, half cross stitch when worked with heavy rug yarn on twisted double-thread canvas saves time and yarn and does not pull the canvas excessively out of shape. A lining or a rug pad is recommended for all needlepoint and embroidered rugs. Close straight or diagonal stitches, with an equal amount of yarn on both the front and the back of the foundation fabric, are excellent space or edge fillers. A zigzagging jacquard arrangement of diagonal stitches works up rapidly and provides texture in a single- or two-color design. Looped embroidery stitches and many weaving knots produce raised surfaces that are long-wearing and sturdy. These stitches adapt easily to jute and other types of cord.

TURKEY WORK/RYA KNOT/GHIORDES KNOT

This knot can be embroidered on fabric, worked on canvas mesh, or wrapped around warp threads. It is the knot used on almost all Oriental rugs and on Scandinavian rya rugs. Use it as a needle-and-thread addition to wall hangings in need of enrichment or variety, or as a fringe border. Recognize it as the lark's head knot used in macramé work. Use single or multiple threads in the needle.

ON A FABRIC FOUNDATION

Insert the needle through the fabric from the front at A, make a short horizontal stitch to the left across the back, and bring the needle up again on the front surface, at B. Hold down the tail end of the yarn the desired length with the thumb of the other hand. Bring the yarn over the top of the needle and insert the needle horizontally from right to left at C. Bring the needle up a bit to the right of the tail end, at D.

Draw the thread through and down, holding down a length equal to the tail end with the thumb. Insert the needle at E and bring it up again at F, making

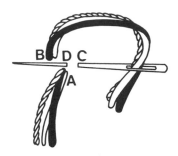

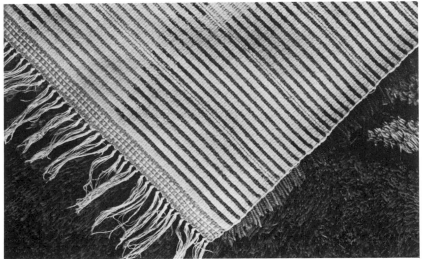

Scandinavian backing woven with finished edges and spaces for turkey work

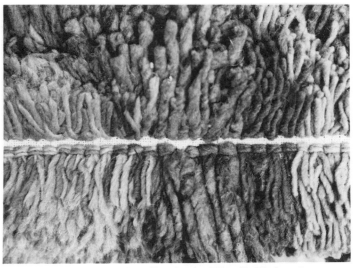

Turkey work embroidered on Duraback cloth with Mexican homespun yarn

Turkey work on fabric

Embroidered turkey-work pillow tops by Gunnel Teitel

169

Turkey work on canvas

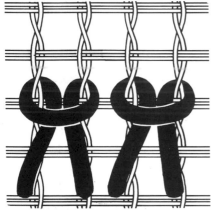

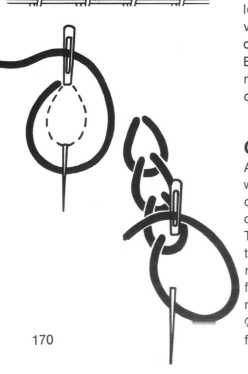

Turkey work embroidered on drawn-thread Duraback for a hearth rug by the author

a short horizontal stitch toward the center of the knot, from right to left. Draw the needle through, maintaining the loop under the thumb. With the thread above the needle, take another short horizontal stitch to the left. Draw the thread down as before. Rows of turkey work can be left looped and uncut for one effect, or may be cut individually. If the loops are to be cut, do each row as soon as it is completed before starting the next one.

ON A CANVAS FOUNDATION

Right-handed people starting the Ghiordes knot or rya knot from the right side will produce exactly the same effect as left-handed people starting from the left. The stitch is perfectly symmetrical. Insert the needle and thread under a vertical warp thread. Hold the tail end down with the thumb. Bring the yarn up, over, around, and under the next parallel warp thread. Pull the needle down. Bring the needle up, inserting it under the next parallel warp thread. As you move from one knot to the next, maintain the length of the loop with the thumb of the other hand.

CHAIN STITCH

A great many early-American carpets were embroidered in chain stitch, as were table covers and draperies for windows and tester beds. Although the chain appears as a wide loop in the diagram in order to show its construction clearly, rows are actually placed close to each other to form a solid surface. This stitch is worked on a fabric foundation. Place a small knot on the end of the yarn to start the first rows. Succeeding lengths of yarn can be started by running a bit of yarn up from the back of the fabric. Take a short straight stitch forward, bringing the yarn around and under the point of the needle. Draw the needle through. Start the next stitch inside the loop of the previous stitch. Chain stitches are maneuverable, fluidly following curved lines and easily filling small circular areas.

BRAIDED CHAIN STITCH

This version of the chain stitch is thick and opaque. It is durable and very useful as a background and filler stitch. Begin the first step in the same manner as the plain chain stitch. Make a small straight stitch, tying down the first loop. Bring the needle up a short distance from the straight stitch. Run the needle behind the first loop without catching any of the background fabric. Bring the needle down very close to where it emerged, bringing the point up again a short distance straight ahead. Now bring the needle up and draw it through the small straight stitch that was used to lock the first loop. Never catch any of the background fabric when drawing the needle through the loops. Do not pull too tightly. Continue advancing the chain and drawing the yarn through the previous loop. The looping can be worked from the left or the right side. This stitch is best worked with the fabric on a stretcher. If you work it without a stretcher, keep the loops loose and block the work after completing it.

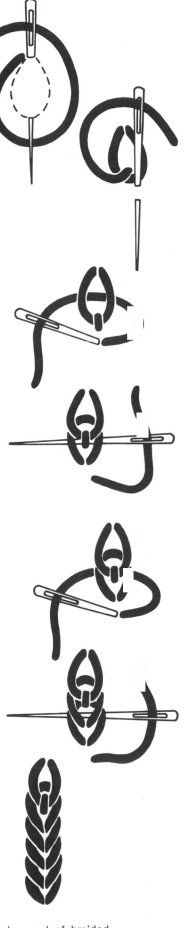

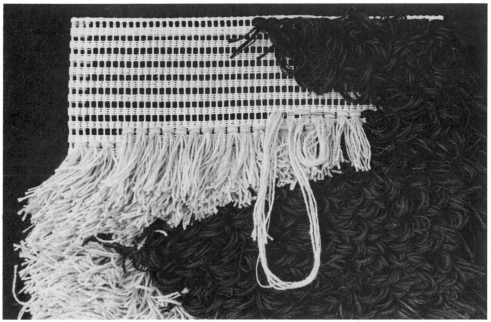

Turkey work embroidered on canvas mesh

The hearth rug shown opposite, finished with a background of braided chain stitch, with a border design adapted from a Persian plate

171

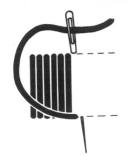

Satin stitch

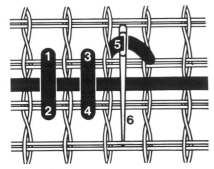

Upright Gobelin stitch

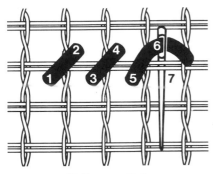

Half cross stitch

STRAIGHT SATIN STITCH/UPRIGHT GOBELIN STITCH

Straight stitches placed close together form a serviceable opaque filling stitch known as satin stitch. For a full effect, do not pull the stitches too tightly. Very long stitches may snag and appear loose. Place stitches next to each other without overlapping. Row upon row of evenly spaced straight stitches have the look of corduroy.

Worked on rug canvas with very heavy yarn, the straight stitch is known as the upright Gobelin stitch because it resembles the weave of this famous tapestry. Work over two weft threads, bringing the needle up from between two warp threads at the top or bottom of the row. Turn the canvas for each row. Keep the needle movements uniform throughout for an even appearance. Use heavy three-ply rug yarn on five-mesh canvas for coverage. For a raised effect and more complete coverage, the stitch can be padded by laying a long horizontal thread on the canvas and carrying it along under the upright stitches.

HALF CROSS STITCH

Half cross stitch is a perennial favorite because it is uncomplicated, adapts well to small, intricate designs, and uses less wool than many other needlepoint stitches. The correct choice of canvas mesh size is very important for detailed designs. Although three and four mesh spaces to the inch work up very rapidly, the effect is coarse, gradation of color becomes crude, and areas intended to curve gently are jagged. A twisted double-thread five-mesh canvas is suitable to a broad design interpretation for a rug, particularly a large rug. Work from left to right, bringing the needle up at the bottom of the stitch. Cross diagonally over one mesh intersection of the canvas, inserting the needle in the row above. Bring the needle point up in the opening directly below. Turn the work upside down so that the next row can be worked from left to right. Persian wool is composed of three single strands. To cover the canvas, it must be used doubled over, or six single strands must be used together. Persian wool is available in hundreds of tints and tones of different hues. It is most convenient to use for small design areas, particularly floral designs with many leaves and tendrils. Areas of Persian yarn mix well with areas of rug yarn of similar ply. Large backgrounds can be filled with less expensive yarn bought in bulk.

Needlepoint rug designed by Gunnel Teitel for a Girl Scout project
Design is based on American Indian yei figures

Hooked and embroidered pillow by Pat Newman

A

B

C

D

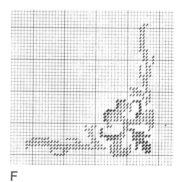

E

F

Stages in the development of a rug made in sections:
A. The test square. B. The test square corrected for
heightened contrast. C. Varying the design, using only
a simple wreath of the leafy background. D. Assembling
the blocks. E. The meeting of the borders forms a new
design. F. Plotting a corner of the border on graph
paper.

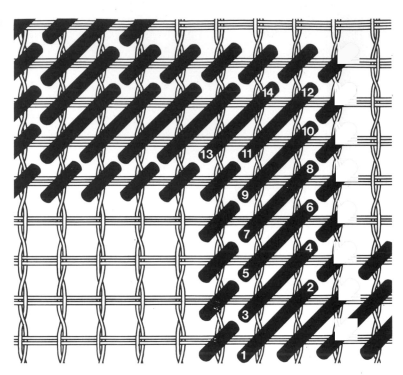

Jacquard stitch

JACQUARD STITCH

This combination of half cross stitches and longer diagonal stitches adds texture to large flat areas with little or no design elements. The zigzagging is most effective when done over a fairly large area. Work diagonally in steps from the bottom right upward to the left, alternating rows of half cross stitch with diagonal half cross stitches taken over two mesh intersections. Move upward six stitches and across six stitches. The stitch can be worked in one or more colors.

CROSS STITCH

The basic cross stitch gives good coverage and can be worked over one or two intersections, depending upon the size of the canvas. A row can be completed by making half cross stitches and then working back in the opposite direction. However, there is always less distortion of the canvas when the stitches are completed individually. Stitches can be worked from the left or the right but must always cross in the same direction for a consistently even appearance.

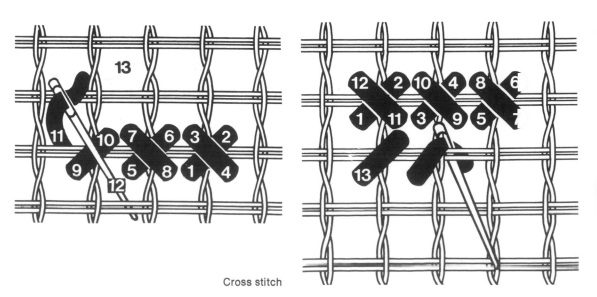

Cross stitch

Victorian cross-stitch detail

Loop stitch

LOOP STITCH

Many embroidery stitches can be either adapted to canvas or worked on a fabric foundation. Loop stitch is very effective in jute on a four-mesh canvas. For a regular appearance without ridges, start each row anew from the right or the left if the work was started from the left. The stitch is worked vertically with the loop over the center mesh; therefore start in the center of a three-mesh space. Bring the needle up from the back and cross the intersection diagonally upward to the left. Bring the yarn straight down across the back, bringing it up again in the third space. Draw the yarn up to the left and insert the needle under the half cross stitch without going under the mesh. The yarn is now in position to start the next stitch. If wool is used, insert the needle in the next space to the left of 2. With heavier cord, skip a space.

Loop-stitch embroidery on rug canvas by Eleanor Bello. Design by the author

Steps in making
the Asian cross
stitch on canvas

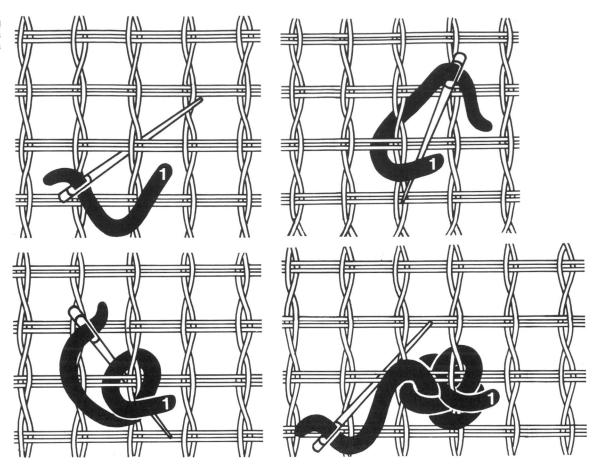

ASIAN CROSS STITCH

A sea-grass mat knotted in Taiwan inspired this stitch. It forms a perfect cross stitch on the reverse side. Heavy three-ply rug yarn on four-mesh canvas makes a very sturdy rug. If jute is used, skip one mesh intersection between knots. 1. Bring the yarn up in a space and slip the needle *upward* under the mesh intersection above, from the left side. 2. Bring the yarn around the intersection and under the loop without picking up the mesh. 3. Bring the yarn up to the left again, insert the needle *downward* under the mesh intersection, and draw the yarn up under the new loop. 4. Start the next stitch two meshes to the left.

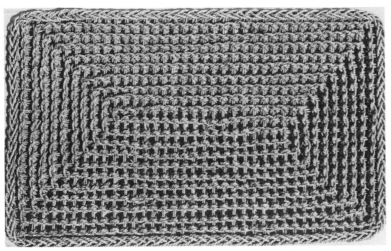

Knotted sea-grass mat from Taiwan from which the Asian cross-stitch was adapted

Detail of mat from Taiwan

STARTING AND FINISHING YARNS

Needlepoint and embroidery yarns should be started without knots wherever possible. Usually, running the yarn over and under the canvas threads for about 1½″ and then working back over it will lock the starting yarn in securely. A knot can be placed on the end of the yarn before it is run through six or seven intersections (provided it does not fall through the large spaces) and should then be cut off after the running stitches have been covered. The knot could be placed in the hem allowance on embroidery and cut off before the hem is turned. Once the yarn is started, new threads can be run through the stitches on the reverse side. End the yarn by running it through the stitches on the back. Heavy jute is something of a problem. One solution is to divide the end of the jute strand in half and tie a square knot. The jute ends can be pulled through other stitches on the reverse side. If all else fails, a drop of white glue will secure the ends.

JOINING NEEDLEPOINT SECTIONS

Sections are joined from the right side or front of the work. Fold back the hem allowance of the canvas on the warp thread so that the top and bottom spaces line up perfectly. Place the two sections side by side and match the weft threads of the two sections to be joined. Check the weft and the spaces of the two pieces along the entire length. There may be some distortion in the canvas, necessitating easing in of one section. Match all design sections. With needle and sewing cotton baste the two sections together, using the half cross stitch and yarn of the background color. Carefully adjust the canvas and work over the basting thread with yarn matching the background color. Follow the direction and type of the background stitches. The raw edges on the reverse side can be secured by overcasting them to the stitching and covering them with seam binding for additional security.

177

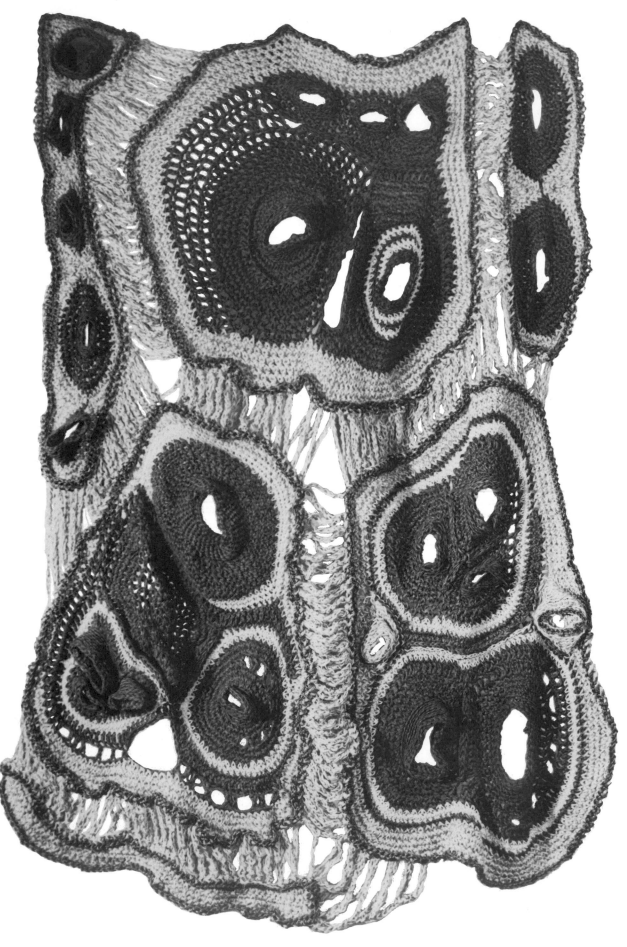

Soft Sea by Maggi Jo Norton. Crocheted of jute in sections and joined with lengths of
chain stitches—a design inspired by patterns of waves and foam receding from rocks

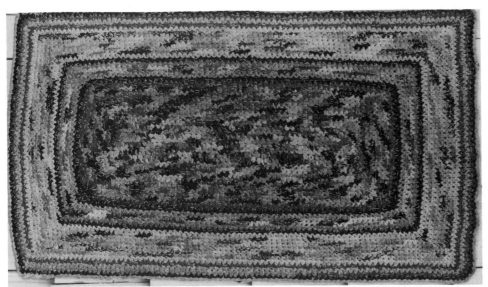

Crocheted rag rug in Hit-or-Miss pattern with cord added for extra strength. Collection Mr. and Mrs. Andrew Geller

CROCHETED AND KNITTED RUGS AND WALL HANGINGS

THE HISTORICAL ORIGINS of knitting and crocheting are rather vague, perhaps because these crafts have been so long in common use. Chaining, looping, and the interlinking of fibers are universal and ageless techniques. Peruvians were masters of many types of linking methods that appear to be knitting, but with a slightly different twist. The forms of knitting stitches as we know them today are evident in the laces and embroideries worn by the wealthy in the fifteenth century in Italy and Spain; the peasants probably knitted for their own use as well. No doubt knitting and crochet needles evolved naturally from the use of common sticks or bones as an aid in forming the web faster and more efficiently. The desire for comfortable hosiery was so great that its manufacture by hand knitting, already a highly skilled craft in the sixteenth century, was amplified by the invention of a knitting machine by William Lee in 1589, during the reign of Elizabeth I. "Stocking stitch" or "stockinet stitch" are terms that aptly describe a primary function of plain knitting. Crochet is the French word for hook, and *tricoter à crochet,* as the French describe crocheting, simply means to knit with a hook. Tricot, in both French and English, is knitted work done either by hand or by machine.

Wall hangings and rugs created by artist-craftsmen have taken a new turn with the revival of these old forms. Knitting has tremendous flexibility and a fluidity that few other construction techniques can surpass; like Topsy, it just grows and grows, and can do so in most any direction. Craftsmen concerned with three-dimensionality experiment with the possibilities of trapunto and padded work done in the round, and with the incredible ruffles that can flow forth from the crochet hook. Their new tapestries have brought the medium in one fell swoop from the classical to the baroque.

Any type of material, from rags to the riches of gold filament, can be knitted or crocheted. The simplest stitches in the coarsest materials make the best rugs. The knitting and crocheting of rugs flowered during the deepest Depression years of the 1930s. Favorite patterns were granny squares and Hit-or-Miss stripes, because they could be accumulated from odd bits of yarn of diverse colors. These patterns should be worked in yarns or fibers that are all of comparable weight and good quality, for even wear and durability.

179

CROCHETING

There are many possible arrangements of the basic crochet stitch. The detailed examples given here are suggested for their variety, versatility, and adaptability to room interiors. Any or all of these stitches can be used for wall hangings in conjunction with single and double crochet stitches.

GLOSSARY

CROCHET HOOK

The hook is used to grasp the yarn and pull it through loops. A hook of the correct size will grasp and hold the yarn without splitting the fibers.

SLIP KNOT

The looped knot that starts the chain stitch.

CHAIN STITCH

A series of loops made by pulling each loop through the preceding loop.

GAUGE

This term refers to the number of stitches per inch. To figure gauge, take a 2″ square sample and count the number of stitches and rows produced by a specific yarn and hook. (Jute samples should be at least 4″ square.) Multiply the number of stitches in an inch by the number of inches required by your design or pattern.

SINGLE CROCHET

The linking of rows of loops to form a flexible but firm, tight fabric.

YARN-OVER

An extra loop of yarn drawn over the hook without inserting the hook in the previous row.

DOUBLE CROCHET

A doubled loop that produces more open spacing between rows.

SLIP STITCH

A utility stitch for joining rings and rows, advancing to a new position, and ending the work.

Ancient Egypt by Maggi Jo Norton. Crocheted wall hanging in wool and gold thread with additional embroidery

180

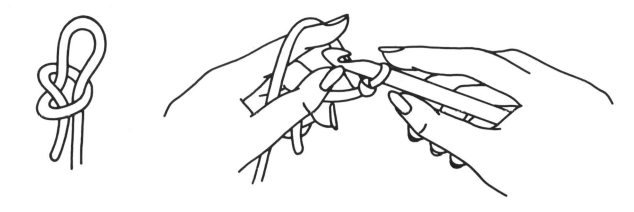

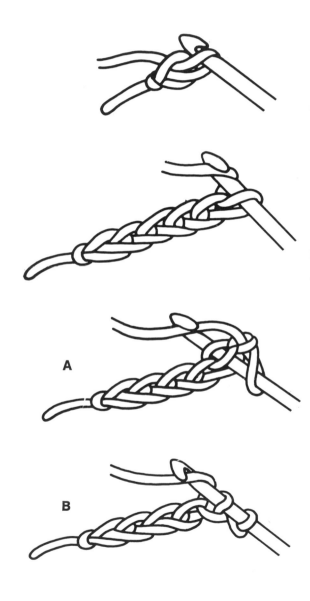

SLIP KNOT

Make an open loop near the end of the yarn. Hold the bottom of the loop firmly between thumb and forefinger. With the other hand, bring the long end of the yarn around behind the loop. Draw the yarn up through the loop, forming a second loop. Pull up the short end of the yarn, tightening the first loop.

CHAIN STITCH

Place the crochet hook in the slip-knot loop. Bring the yarn over the hook and draw it through the loop, forming another loop. Repeat until the desired length is reached.

SINGLE CROCHET (Double Crochet in Great Britain)

A. Start back at the end of the chain by placing the crochet hook with the last chain loop on it under the top loop of the second chain from the hook.

B. Hold the yarn over the index finger of your other hand. Grasp the yarn at the back with the hook and pull up another loop. Bring the yarn over the hook again.

C. Pull the yarn through both loops to complete a single crochet stitch.

When you come to the end of the row, chain one to turn the row before starting the next row of single crochet. On the second and subsequent rows the hook goes into the top two threads of the stitch below.

DOUBLE CROCHET (Treble Crochet in Great Britain)

A. Take the yarn over the hook.
B. Insert the hook under the top loop of the fourth chain from the hook.
C. There are now three loops on the hook.
D. Take the yarn over the hook and draw it through two of the three loops. There will be two loops left on the hook.
E. Take the yarn over the hook again and draw it through both loops. The double crochet stitch is complete when one loop is left on the hook.

When you come to the end of a row of double crochet, chain three before starting the next row. This allows room for the new row to build up. On the return row, remember that the chain is there, and do not crochet into it.

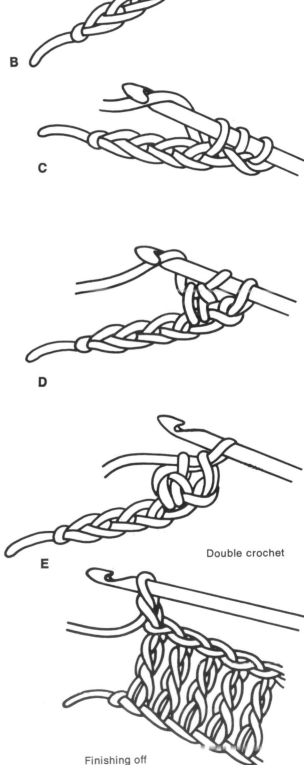

SLIP STITCH (Single Crochet in Great Britain)

Slip stitch is used to close a circle of chain stitches, to advance to a new position, or as a finishing stitch. Insert the crochet hook under the top loops of the last stitch, take the yarn over the hook, and draw the yarn through the top loops and the loop on the hook.

FINISHING OFF

Complete the last stitch. Take the yarn over the hook and draw it through the loop on the hook. Cut the yarn several inches from the loop and draw the cut end through the loop.

Crocheting may be worked back and forth in rows, like knitting, or may be done in continuous rounds, to make circles and ovals. Combinations of stitches done in continuous rounds will produce a variety of curved or angular forms, including the granny square.

GRANNY SQUARES

The traditional granny square consists of five rounds of crocheting. The symmetrically designed motif is a complete unit, which can be enlarged by adding rounds. These units, when joined together, become a related part of the whole. Unusual arrangements can be made by mixing the sizes of the units. For instance, two 4″ squares will line up along the side of an 8″ square. Irregular spacing can be filled with rows of single crochet stitches. As the squares accumulate, check them against each other to maintain the correct size. Use colors with verve, or try the subtle recessive colors of natural materials.

GRANNY SQUARES WORKED IN FOUR COLORS

Always work with the right side facing you.
Starting at the center, with color A, make a slip knot and chain 6. Join with a slip stitch to form a ring.

ROUND 1   Chain 3, work 2 double crochet stitches into the center of the ring, chain 2. * Work 3 double crochet stitches in the ring, chain 2. Repeat from * three times. Join with a slip stitch to the top of chain. Cut the end of the thread 2″ away from the slip stitch and pull the end through the loop of the slip stitch.

ROUND 2   Attach color B to the crochet hook with a slip knot, bring the yarn over the hook, hold the two loops on the hook with the index finger, and insert the hook in any one of the four chain 1 spaces. Draw up loop and complete a double crochet stitch. Work 2 more double crochet stitches in the same space and chain 2. Add 3 more double crochets in same space and chain 1 to complete the first corner. Work 3 double crochets, chain 2 and work 3 double crochets,

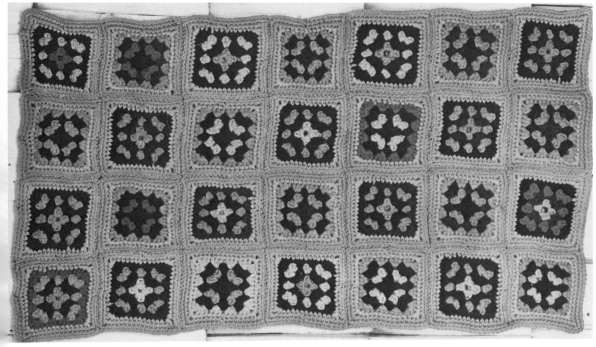

Multicolored Granny Square carpet, 1930. Collection Mr. and Mrs. Andrew Geller

chain 1 in each of the next three spaces to complete the four corners. Join with a slip stitch. Cut the end of the thread 2″ away from the slip stitch and pull the end through the loop of the slip stitch.

ROUND 3   Attach color C to the crochet hook with a slip knot, bring the yarn over the hook and insert the hook in a corner space. Draw up a loop and complete the double crochet stitch. Work 2 more double crochet stitches in the same space, chain 2. Work 3 more double crochet stitches in the same space and chain 1 to complete the corner.

In the next space work 3 double crochets, chain 1. Work around the square, placing 2 sets of 3 double crochet stitches in each corner, chaining 2 in the middle and 1 at the end of each set, and placing 1 set of double crochet stitches in each side space.

ROUND 4   Attach color D in a corner space and work around the square as before, placing 2 sets of 3 double crochets (chaining 1 at the end of each double set) in each corner and 1 set in each of the 2 side spaces.

Repeat these rounds in any color or combination of colors for any desired size square. If you wish to work the rounds in one color for more than one round do not break off the thread. Slip stitch in each stitch to the place where the next round begins, and chain 3 if the next stitch is a double crochet. Chain 2 if the next stitch is a single crochet stitch. After the pattern has been completed, rounds of single crochet can be used to increase the size of each square.

ASSEMBLING AND JOINING SQUARES

Arrange the accumulated squares on a flat surface before joining. Consider the plan carefully, fitting and rearranging the squares until the color scheme is satisfactory. Crochet or sew the squares together. Use a blunt yarn needle for sewing. Work from the wrong side, lacing back and forth from edge to edge, with matching yarn for an invisible finish. To crochet the squares together, use a slip stitch on the reverse side, using only the top loop of each stitch for a flat finish, or single crochet the squares together on the front surface, to effect a decorative ridge around each square.

Round puff-stitch rug, 1930.
Courtesy Visa Johnston

Puff-stitch hexagonal rug. Detail. Collection of the author

PUFF STITCHES FORMING A HEXAGON

"Fast, plump, and effective" best describes the crocheted puff stitch hexagon rug. For easy washing use two strands of acrylic yarn as one. One-strand three-ply wool rug yarn works equally well, with more care in washing. Practice the puff stitch in order to become acquainted with the tension, the length of stitch, the number of loops that must be held on the crochet hook. Use a single color, a tricolor scheme, or use two strands together, mixing the colors for a tweedy effect. Work with the right side facing you. Make a slip knot and chain 4. Join with a slip stitch to form a ring. Chain 1.

ROUND 1   With the yarn over the hook, insert hook into the ring, bring the yarn over the hook and pull through the ring. You will have 3 loops on the hook. (Work loosely, making long loops. Do not pull up tight.) Repeat 3 more times for a total of 9 long loops on the hook. Yarn over the hook and pull yarn through all of the loops on the hook, including the original chain loop. Chain 1. This is the completed puff stitch. Repeat 5 more times, finishing with 6 puff stitches in the chain ring. Slip stitch into the chain stitch on top of the first puff worked to complete the ring of 6 puffs.

ROUND 2   Chain 1. With the yarn over the hook, insert hook into the space formed between the 6th and the 1st puff. Yarn over and pull through. Finish the puff. Repeat to form a second puff in the same space. Place 2 puff stitches in each space, to increase the diameter of the round. There will be 12 puff stitches in this round. Slip stitch into the chain of the 1st puff stitch in this row.

ROUND 3   Chain 1, yarn over, and insert hook into the space formed by the last and 1st puff stitch of the previous row. Yarn over and pull through. Make only 1 puff in this space. In the next space make 2 puffs, then 1, then 2, alternating around the row. End with 2 puffs and slip stitch into the chain of the 1st starting puff.

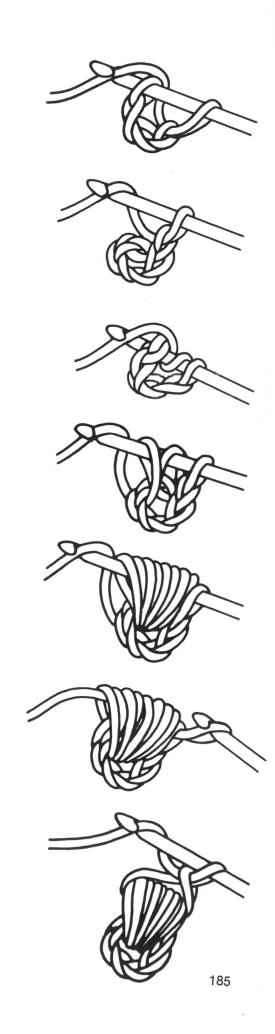

185

ROUND 4   Chain 1, yarn over, insert hook into the space formed by the last and the 1st puff stitch of the previous row. Again make only one puff stitch in the 1st space, then another single puff stitch in the next space, followed by 2 puff stitches in the next space. Follow this rhythm: 1, 1, 2, 1, 1, 2, 1, 1, 2, until the row is completed.

ROUND 5   Increase 1 single puff, in this order: 1, 1, 1, 2, 1, 1, 1, 2, 1, 1, 1, 2, until the row is completed.

Follow the pattern of increasing 1 single puff between double puffs each round. The double puffs occur over each other to form the 6 radiating spokes of the hexagon. Increase each round until the desired diameter is reached.

Make fringe tassels from multiple 9″ ends of yarn. Insert the ends in each space between puffs and tie with a lark's head knot.

CROCHETED LOOPED PILE

A very good pile rug can be crocheted as well as woven. A small practice sample of looping should be made in order to learn how to position your fingers in the most comfortable way. How to hold the yarn conveniently in both knitting and crocheting is a very personal matter. Making a sample will help you to determine the right spacing between rows of loops for the type of yarn you have selected. The rows of looping are alternated with rows of either single or double crochet, so that the loops will appear on only one side of the piece. A row of single crochet stitches between loops will result in a heavier pile, while a row of double crochet stitches results in a slightly sparser pile. This stitch can be worked in sections from 1' to 18" wide and slip stitched or whipped together. Another method of joining is to work very wide strips about 1' long. Butt the strips together in sets of two, finished top edge to finished top edge, so that the loops of the first strip face the left and the loops of the other strip face the right. This will look like a stripe of flat crocheting. Join two, four, six, or more sets in this manner. Whether you space the rows of loops between rows of single crochet or double crochet, or alternate rows of single and double crochet, start with a row of double crochet. Although separate strips that are to be attached to each other may end with a row of single crochet, the ultimate ending of the rug or wall hanging should be a row of double crochet to match the start.

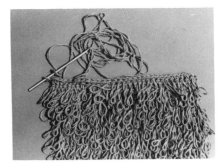

Looped pile in single crochet

Looped pile in double crochet

Extending the yarn to make loops

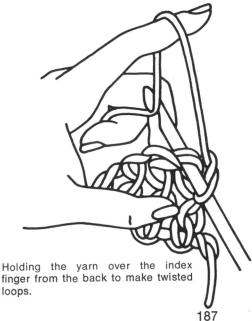

Holding the yarn over the index finger from the back to make twisted loops.

Make a slip knot and chain the desired length. Heavy rug yarn chained with a J or #10 crochet hook will make about three chain stitches per inch.

ROW 1 Make a row of double crochet stitches, chain 1, and turn to the reverse side. All the loops will fall on the side now turned away from you.

ROW 2 Twist the yarn around your pinkie and hold it up on your extended index finger. Place the thumb on the side facing you, with the last three fingers holding the piece on the back. Insert the hook in the space under the top chain of the double crochet and grasp the yarn at the other end of the loop, below the extended index finger. (Note: If the yarn is held over the extended

187

index finger from the front of the finger, the loops will hang without plying around each other; if the yarn is lifted over the back of the index finger, the loops will twist around themselves. Long loops that are plied in this way are less likely to snag.) Holding the loop taut, pull the yarn through and make a single crochet without pulling up the long loop. Drop the loop from the index finger, draw up another loop with the index finger and start the next stitch. End the row with chain 1 if you intend to use a row of single crochet stitches on the next row, or chain 3 if the next row will consist of double crochet stitches. Turn the work.

ROW 3 Complete a row of single or double crochet stitches according to the spacing between rows of loops.

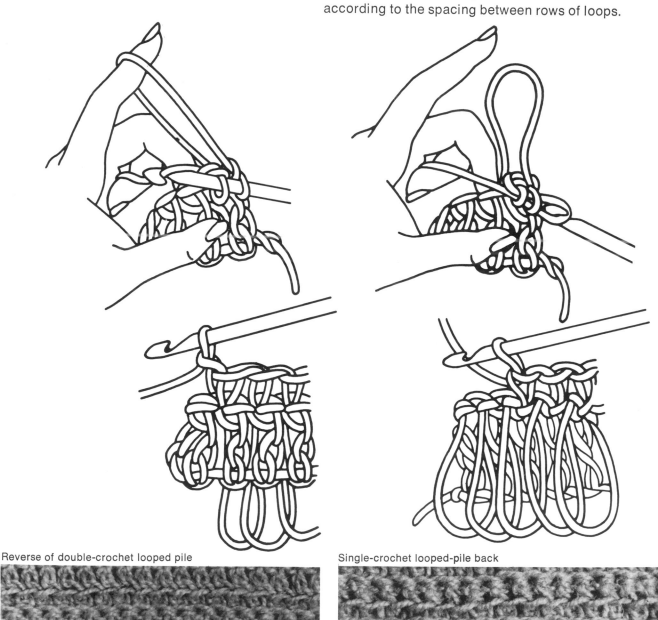

Reverse of double-crochet looped pile

Single-crochet looped-pile back

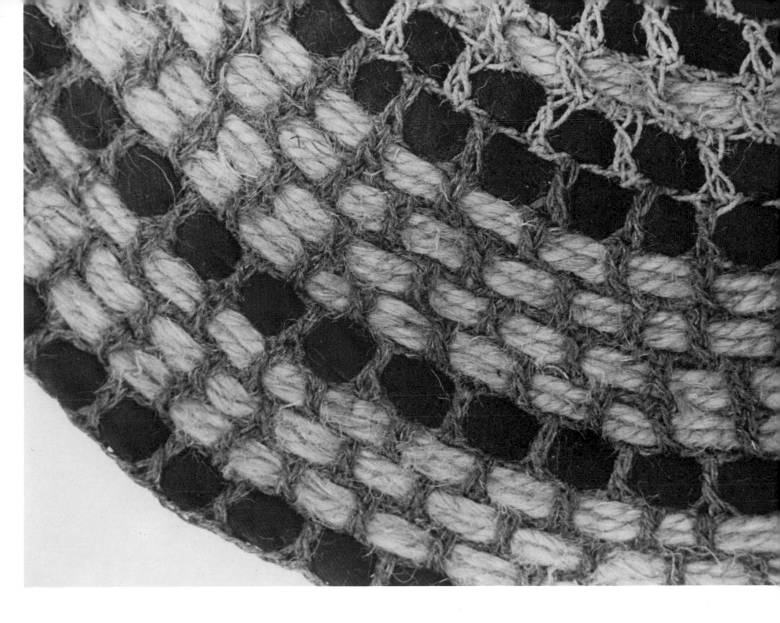

FILET MESH

Filet mesh produces an open lattice. Almost any type of material may be laced through the spaces. Heavy jute, strips of leather or vinyl, terry cloth toweling, fur, or nylon stockings may be woven through the crocheted base. Decorative meshes of raffia or metallic threads make interesting wall hangings when laced with dried thistles, straw flowers, cattails, or other natural materials.

Make a slip knot and chain the desired length. The mesh may be started in a base row of single crochet stitches or directly in the chain. A wall hanging made of heavyweight cordage interlaced with leather and jute is more contemporary in effect if left without little edges of single crochet. The large open mesh is worked in double crochet stitches. The spaces are created by making a specific number of chain stitches and skipping the same number of stitches in the previous row, then working a double crochet to hold the meshes together.

ROW 1 If a base row of single crochet is used, chain 4 and turn. Otherwise add 4 chains to the measurement of the base chain and turn the work.

ROW 2 Place 1 double crochet in the third stitch of a previous row of single crochet, or in the sixth chain from the

189

Filet mesh

hook on a base chain. Chain 1. Skip the next stitch of the previous row. Make 1 double crochet stitch in the stitch after the one skipped. Continue across the row in this manner. Chain 5 and turn.

Work back across the row; place each double crochet in the one directly below. At the end of a row, chain 1 after the next to the last double crochet and place the final double crochet in the second chain stitch of the turning chain, skipping the last double crochet of the previous row. If you work with a starting chain instead of a row of single crochet, the chain stitches would have to be calculated accurately to end up with an even amount of open boxes. If you find that extra stitches are left on the end of the chain, just open the slip knot, remove the extra stitches carefully, and pull up the tail end of the yarn.

Open filet mesh of polished Italian marine jute laced with doubled three-ply jute

Open filet mesh laced with jute. Jute ends are wrapped with masking tape to facilitate lacing

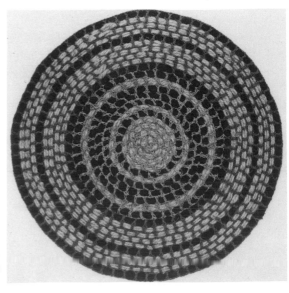

Circular filet mesh laced alternately with doubled jute and bias strips cut from worn black tricot slacks

Tambour crocheted rug or wall hanging by Eleanor Bello

TAMBOUR CHAIN CROCHET

CHAINING WITH A CROCHET HOOK on a felted or loosely woven background is usually considered an embroidery stitch. In Eastern countries today, particularly Iraq and India, it is used as a rapid way of embroidering large areas in chain stitch. This technique is usually worked on a stretched, taut surface. Embroideries from Turkestan are worked with very fine hooks in many-colored designs of great intricacy. Each minute chain stitch measures about $1/16''$. Crochet chain stitches can be worked on almost any fabric and on needlepoint mesh canvas. The yarn must be suitable to the size of the hook, and of course the fabric should have an open weave that will allow the crochet hook to pass through easily. A great many pillows and rugs from India are decorated with tambour chain work in specific design areas, leaving much of the background fabric exposed.

CHAINING

Hold the yarn under the backing fabric, push the crochet hook through from the front surface, grasp the yarn and pull a loop through to the top. Advance the hook and push it through the fabric again, pulling up another loop on the hook. Pull this loop through the first one to complete a chain. No knot is needed to start the chaining. To finish the chain cut the yarn beneath the fabric and pull the end up through the center of the last loop, then down through the fabric by grasping it from beneath the fabric with the crochet hook. Tie an overhand knot on the end.

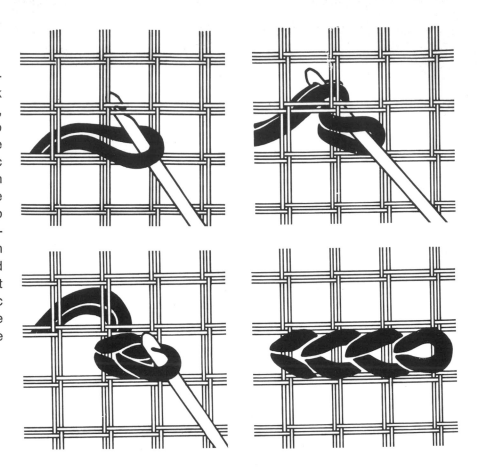

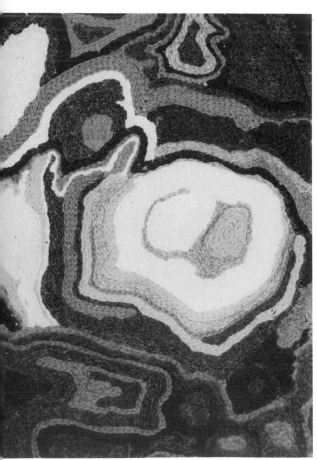

Tambour crochet on monk's cloth by Maggi Jo Norton. Design inspired by an aerial photograph of a landscape

Indian carpet in tambour chain embroidered on hand-woven fabric with a crochet hook. Collection of the author

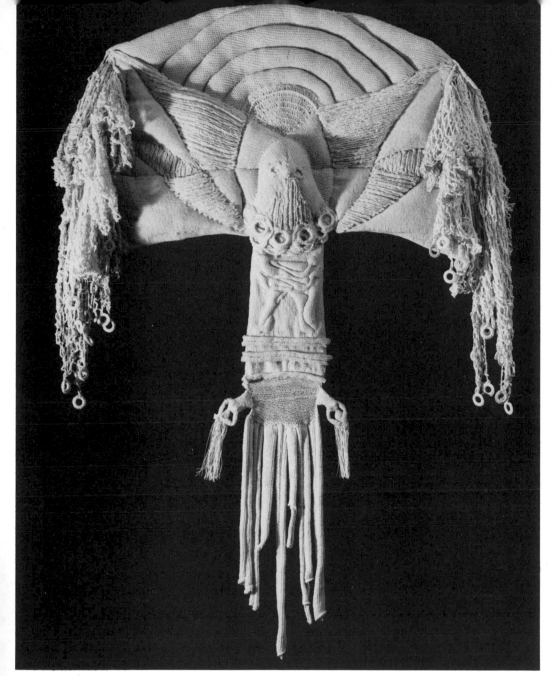

Bird of Prey by Norma Minkowitz. Knitted, crocheted, trapunto-padded wall hanging. Photo Kobler/Dyer Studios

KNITTING

ALMOST ANY ONE OF HUNDREDS of knitting stitches can be used for wall hangings. However, one must be more practical in choosing stitches for rugs. Reversible stitches are quite satisfactory, not necessarily just because they are reversible, but because stitches such as garter and seed stitch produce a thick, raised surface of firm substance.

GLOSSARY

KNITTING NEEDLES
Heavy-gauge needles of substantial length are practical.

CASTING ON
Putting the starting stitches on the needle.

KNITTING

Inserting the needle through the front of the stitch, *from front to back,* keeping the yarn at the *back* of the work.

PURLING

Inserting the needle under the front of the stitch, *from back to front,* with the yarn at the *front.*

CASTING ON USING ONE NEEDLE

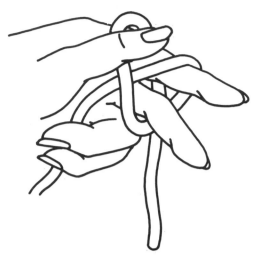

Form a slip knot on the needle by holding the measured amount of yarn over the palm of the hand, bringing it over and around the index and third finger. Bring the yarn up and around again.

When using one needle to cast on, a length of yarn sufficient to form the first row of knitting must be drawn from the ball before the slip knot is made. The amount of yarn necessary can be determined by casting on 10 loops. Spread the base of these loops on the needle and measure their width. Draw the loops off the needle, opening them to their fullest length before measuring the amount of yarn with a ruler. Write the two sets of figures down on paper and calculate the amount needed by determining how many loops are necessary for the desired width. For instance, if 10 loops measure 2″ in width, 6 × 10 loops, or 60 loops, would be needed for a 1′ width. Therefore 6 times the fully extended length of yarn, plus a bit extra for the slip knot, would be necessary for casting on the loops. Always cast on loosely.

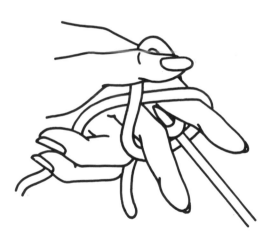

Draw a loop from between the index and third finger.

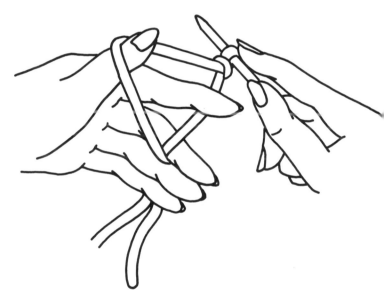

Tighten the slip knot by inserting the thumb and index finger between the strands and spreading the fingers.

Pick the loop up directly onto the needle.

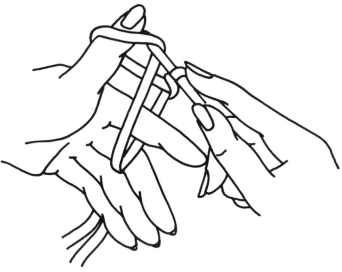

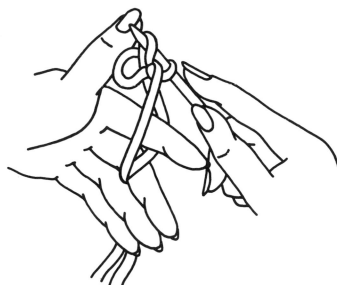

With both ends held between the third and fourth fingers for tension, insert the thumb and index finger between the two strands of yarn so that the measured end is extended over the thumb. Bring the needle to the outside of the thumb. Insert the point of the needle from front to back under the loop on the thumb. Do not remove the loop from the thumb or the needle.

Pull the loop onto the needle through the loop over the thumb. Release the loop over the thumb.

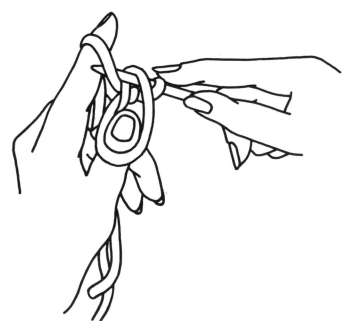

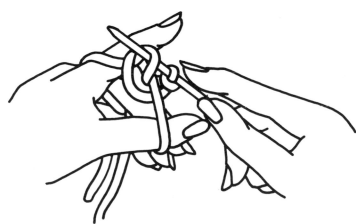

Press the thumb against the strand emerging from the released loop in order to tighten the loop now on the needle.

Insert the needle point under the strand over the index finger from front to back.

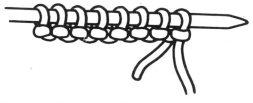

Continue casting on until the desired amount of loops is on the needle.

This method of casting on has two distinct advantages. The slip knot is placed at one end, and as many loops as desired are placed on the needle directly from the ball of yarn. Knitting requires the use of both hands with equal facility. However, left-handers will find casting on with two needles pleasantly effortless.

Begin with a slip knot at the end of the yarn by bringing the end around in a circle and pulling a short loop of the yarn coming from the ball up through the center of the circle. Tighten the loop. Place the loop on a needle held in the left hand.

Insert the right-hand needle through the loop on the needle from front to back and bring the yarn up over the point of the right-hand needle.

Pull the loop through, leaving the slip knot loop on the left-hand needle. The start of the new loop is on the right-hand needle.

Pull out the loop on the right-hand needle a bit to loosen it. Pull back the left-hand needle and bring it forward, inserting the point through the loop on the right-hand needle from front to back and slide the loop to the left-hand needle.

When the new loop is on the left-hand needle, remove the right-hand needle.

FOR A FIRMER FABRIC

Rugs should have a firm fabric without elasticity. To minimize elasticity, insert the needle into the back of the stitch. When you are casting on with two needles, the right-hand needle can be inserted into the back of the loop. There is a slight economy of yarn with this method. All knit stitches can be worked into the back of the stitch, as can the purl stitches. However, one of the two rows must be worked into the front of the stitches.

TO KNIT

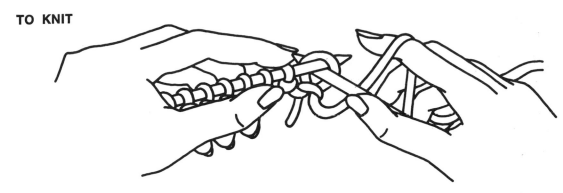

Cast on the required number of stitches. Hold the needle in the left hand. Place the index finger on top of the needle between the first and the second loop. The thumb is held just below the needle, comfortably and a bit back from the position of the index finger. The other fingers are behind the work, supporting the weight of the needle. Insert the right-hand needle through the first loop from front to back.

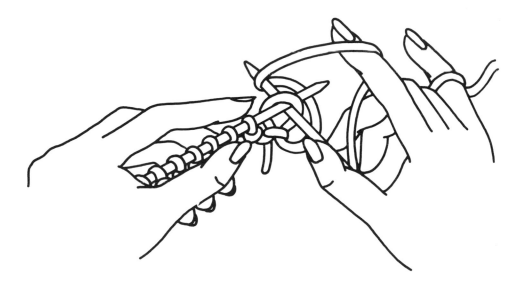

Bring the yarn around to the back and over the right-hand needle.

Draw the loop over the right-hand needle through the loop of the left-hand needle.

Carefully withdraw the right-hand needle with the new loop on it and at the same time drop the old loop off the left-hand needle. Complete the row until all the loops are knitted onto the right-hand needle.

Octopus, knitted pillow-toy in bright primary colors by Jan Silberstein

TO PURL

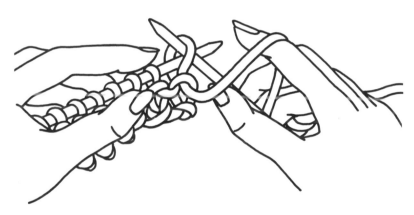

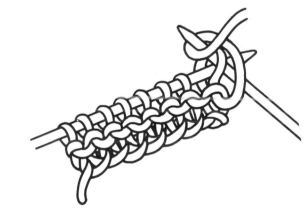

For each new row take the needle from the right hand, turn it around and place it in the left hand. Place the empty needle in the right hand. With the yarn at the front of the work, insert the right-hand needle under the front of the first loop, from back to front.

Draw the yarn from the front up and around the right-hand needle.

Draw the right-hand needle with the new stitch on it through the loop on the left-hand needle.

Slip the old loop off the left-hand needle while pulling up the new loop on the right-hand needle.

BINDING OFF

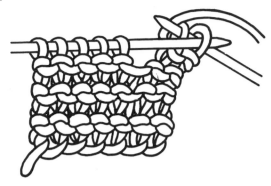

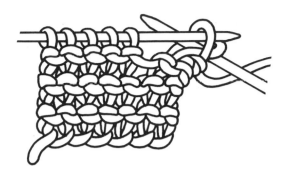

Knit two stitches. Reach over the second stitch with the left-hand needle and insert it in the first stitch made on the right-hand needle.

With the left-hand needle, draw the first stitch over the second stitch.

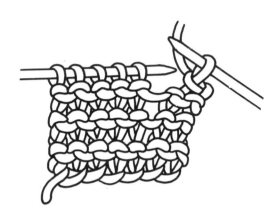

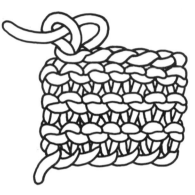

Drop the first stitch. One stitch remains on the right-hand needle.

Knit another stitch. Draw the first loop over the one just knitted and drop it off the needle. Continue across the row, knitting one and dropping one until 1 stitch remains. Cut the yarn about 2″ or 3″ from the end and draw the end through the last loop. Weave the end back into the fabric of the knitting with a crochet hook.

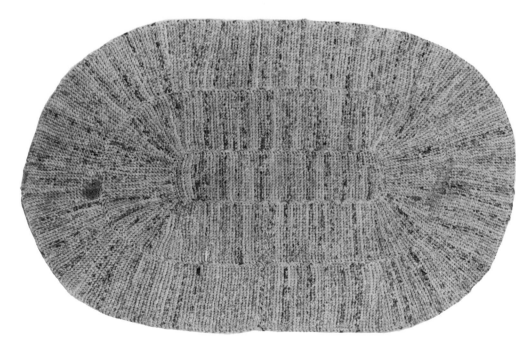

Early rag rug knitted in Hit-or-Miss pattern. Collection Mr. and Mrs. Maurice Vanderwoude

Three-color oval jute rug knitted in garter stitch by Janna Mandel

The great beauty of knitting is its elasticity, splendid for clothing but understandably accounting for its neglect as a means of making rugs. However, materials that do not stretch, such as jute, rags, and some of the polyesters, tightly knitted in reversible stitches, make interesting small rugs. Use large-size knitting needles and make a test sample to determine the gauge (the number of stitches per inch) and the exact size of the needles needed to form a tight knit web suitable to the yarn and practical for use.

KNITTED GARTER STITCH OVAL

This rug was made in sections consisting of a straight center panel surrounded by two oval panels knitted separately and laced together after completion. Coarse three-ply jute and #11 needles were used. The jute was dyed gold, wine, and royal blue. After the addition of fringe the final measurement was 5′ × 6′. The width and the length depend upon the measurement of the central panel, particularly the length. Eleven stitches are cast on for a width of 8½″, and 60 rows are knitted to a length of 21″. The stitch used is called garter stitch, a reversible pattern in which every row is knitted. There are no purl rows. The next oval shape is knitted separately in a straight garter stitch pattern, the same straight width as the central panel, until the approach to the corner where gusset increases are necessary to round the corner in an oval. Start knitting the oval a little below the middle of the center panel. About four rows before the end of the panel, start the increase in four repeats that form the four quarters of the turn:

Detail of the oval rug above

ROW 1. Starting at the outer edge, knit 9 stitches
ROW 2. Knit 9 stitches for the return to the outer edge
ROW 3. Knit 7 stitches
ROW 4. Knit 7 stitches, returning to the outer edge
ROW 5. Knit 4 stitches
ROW 6. Return 4 stitches
ROW 7. Knit 11 stitches
ROW 8. Knit 11 stitches on the return

Repeat steps 1 through 8 three more times. Fit the corner to the bottom of the panel in order to determine how many rows of knitting are needed before the next gusset increase is started.

The next round of the oval is knitted in the same manner. For variety, the width of the rows of garter stitch is increased to 15 stitches. Because the second oval is larger, the size and quantity of stitches is increased in each gusset. Starting at the outside edge with 2 rows of 13 stitches, make 2 rows of 11 stitches, 2 rows of 5 stitches, and finish with 6 rows of 15 stitches. Repeat this gusseting arrangement 6 times to round the oval. Stop frequently to check the fit of the curve to the piece. Each knitter works slightly differently, some more tightly, others loosely. Each type of yarn is different. Strive to keep the ovals lying flat—to do so may require an additional gusset. Work a selvage edge by slipping the first stitch at the beginning of each row onto the needle, then continue to knit as usual.

Sections made of lightweight yarns are best joined by crocheting them together with a slip stitch and yarn of a matching color. Those made of heavyweight yarns such as jute must be laced back and forth with a needle and rug yarn.

SEED STITCH

This stitch, as the name indicates, has a fine-grained texture, much less vigorous than garter stitch in appearance. Cast on an uneven number of stitches. Knit 1, Purl 1, ending with Knit 1. Repeat this sequence throughout.

DOUBLE SEED STITCH

Seed stitch and double seed stitch can be used together in blocks. The double seed stitch is a much livelier pattern that knits up with more regularity. Use it alone or in combination with the seed stitch. It is worked in multiples of 4 plus 2.

ROW 1. Knit 2, Purl 2, alternating across the row, end with Knit 2.
ROW 2. Purl 2, Knit 2, alternating across the row, end with Purl 2.
ROW 3. Purl 2, Knit 2, alternating across the row, end with Purl 2.
ROW 4. Knit 2, Purl 2, alternating across the row, end with Knit 2.
Starting with Row 1, repeat these 4 rows.

These stitches require little or no blocking.

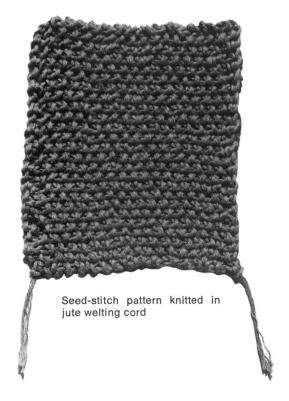

Seed-stitch pattern knitted in jute welting cord

Double seed-stitch pattern knitted in jute welting cord

BRAIDING IS AS OLD A METHOD of rugmaking as rug hooking. As an adornment, braiding was well known all over the ancient world, from Assyria to Egypt, and most certainly among the Indians of America. Braided fringes have been used to tie off the warp ends of woven rugs for centuries.

Sturdy, solid, and firm, braided rugs are appealing for their simplicity and informality. Almost any geometric form is possible: squares, circles, ovals, rectangles. Even stars and their close cousins, the hexagon and the octagon, can be worked out, but design otherwise is limited to the arrangement of color within the braids and in their juxtaposition. The attractive and economical practice of working with worn woolens discourages high-key color schemes and accounts for the predominance of the all-time favorite Hit-or-Miss pattern. If contrasting colors have been used in the three-strand braid, small designs appear voluntarily as the braids are laced together. The popular arrowhead design is formed when two of the three colors used in the braid are the same or similar and the third one provides a contrast. Half of the arrow is formed by a single braid because the two similar colors make a short diagonal within the braid. With careful alignment during lacing, the sections of contrasting color are brought together to form the two halves of the arrowhead. The finest early-American braiders worked with narrow ½″ braids, producing relatively fine-lined chevrons, zigzags, diamonds, and diagonals in their rugs.

MATERIALS

Woolen fabrics are the most satisfactory for braided rugs. Wool resists soil more readily than cotton and produces a plumper braid. Felt and medium-weight woolen flannels of the type often used for hooked rugs are pleasant and convenient to work with. Felt is available in a large assortment of colors. Woolen flannels can readily be dyed to suit a planned color scheme. Old blankets and woolen fabrics of coat weight are the best used materials, provided a sufficient amount of about the same weight is available. Mixing weights will produce an uneven surface. Approximately ¾ pound of fabric will make 1′ square of rug. If you purchase mill ends by the pound, add about 20 per cent because some of the irregular ends may not be useful for braiding. The odd scraps can be used in rug hooking. New and used fabrics are difficult to combine evenly in the same rug. Collect enough fabric before beginning a project in order to plan the color scheme around the materials at hand. Since dyed and undyed fabrics can be used together, always reserve the lighter colors for dyeing. Follow the directions for dyeing woolens given on the packages of good commercial dyes. Prepare used garments before dyeing by ripping open the seams and cutting away unusually worn or moth-eaten sections. Wash worn fabric in lukewarm water with mild soap flakes. Rinse thoroughly. Press, if necessary, as an aid to accurate cutting.

Although precut woolen strips can be purchased from companies specializing in rugmaking supplies, inveterate rug hookers and braiders may find it economical to purchase a cloth cutter with changeable cutter heads. Certain types can be used to cut strips for both hooked and braided rugs by simply changing the cutter head and adjusting the cloth guide.

Heavy cotton or linen carpet thread is needed for lacing the braids together. There are special flat lacing needles called braidkins or bodkins, but a large

BRAIDED RUGS

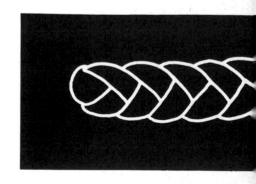

darning or sacking needle is adequate. Clamps are also necessary to hold the finished section of braid so that the strips can be held tautly away from the clamp for working. A clipboard can be used, or a C-clamp attached to the end of a table. Clothespins with wire springs are helpful for holding the braid together when the work is temporarily stopped. However, large paper clips or spring clips are often more easily available.

A set of three Braid-Aids, helpful for turning in the raw edges during braiding, is often considered optional equipment because it turns limited widths. But it does eliminate much of the nuisance work in braiding and is an inestimable timesaver.

GLOSSARY

BRAID
Standard three-strand braid constructed by weaving one strip over another in succession.

BRAID-AID FRONT
A cone-shaped metal device with bent edges for folding strips automatically as they are drawn through the cylinder.

BRAID-AID BACK
Reverse side of the Braid-Aid.

SACKING NEEDLE
Four-inch flattened, curved needle suitable for lacing.

PREPARING STRIPS OF FABRIC
The most important consideration in cutting strips for braiding is to cut with the warp and the weft threads and not on the bias. Cutting on the bias, or diagonally, will cause the strips to stretch thin during braiding. Use a cardboard guide marked with the desired width to cut even strips, or keep a ruler handy to mark the widths before cutting. Use long-bladed, very sharp scissors, or a cloth cutter. Strips are usually cut in widths ranging from 1¼″ to 3″, depending upon the weight of the fabric. Lighter-weight fabrics require wider strips. Do not cut up all of the materials in advance. Cut three strips and braid them before making a final decision on the correct width.

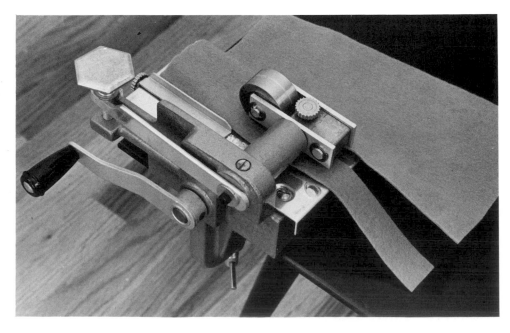

Cutting cloth strips for a braided rug

JOINING THE STRIPS

It is best to join the strips in advance, sewing the short seams on the bias one after another on the sewing machine. They can also be sewn by hand. Place one strip horizontally, right side up. Arrange the strip prepared for joining by overlapping it on the previous strip at a right angle, wrong side up. Sew diagonally across the corner. Cut off the corner 1/8″ away from the stitching. Fold out the vertical strip and press down the stitching with your fingernail. Two strips of the same color may be joined anywhere on a rug, but a new color on a square or rectangular rug must be joined at the corner, so it must be done while the rug is in progress. Fabrics for Hit-or-Miss patterns can be joined at any point, although it is advisable to scatter the spacing of the very dark and very light fabrics throughout, as well as those that are heavily patterned and those without any pattern. Light and dark fabrics can be sorted and grouped for a striped effect. Usually the dark fabrics are reserved for the outer edges.

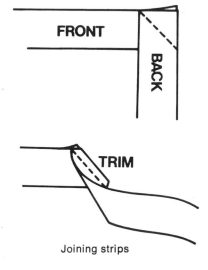

Joining strips

FOLDING THE STRIPS

Turn the raw edges in until they meet in the center, then fold the strips in half. The raw edges will be inside. It is very helpful to blindstitch the edges to hold them together. If the strips are to be dyed after cutting, it is essential to sew them together. Occasionally you may want to add a special color note while the rug is in progress. If the cut strip fits around the perimeter of the rug twice, it will probably be long enough to braid. Experts are able to fold the edges of the strips in with the thumb as they braid, but Braid-Aids are very helpful.

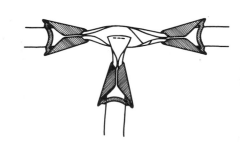

THE T METHOD OF STARTING

If Braid-Aids are used, place them on the unfolded strips by folding or tapering the end of the strip and pushing it through the narrow end of the cone, then down and out of the slit at the bottom. Most Braid-Aids will easily accommodate strips 1½″ wide. Wind up long ends loosely and secure them by running string through the coil and tying it. Unwind the roll as needed. Place Braid-Aids on either end of a straight horizontal strip, the top of the T. Place another strip with a Braid-Aid in the center, halfway between them, at right angles to the top of the T. Place several tacking stitches in the center of the vertical strip. With the Braid-Aids reasonably close, turn down the horizontal strip over the end of the vertical strip. It may be necessary to turn in the top edges of the vertical strip by hand or to blindstitch the starting 2″. Bring up the vertical strip and wrap it around and over the horizontal strip, returning it to its original position. If you use a padded clipboard, pin the top of the braid to the board with a T-pin, until the braid becomes long enough to be held by the clip at the top of the board. The braid can also be held by a C-clamp attached to a board of any kind, or held taut by closing the end into the top of a dresser drawer.

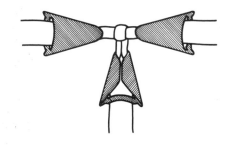

Starting a T

Braiding three strands

THREE-STRAND BRAID

To make a three-strand braid, bring the left-hand side of the top of the T over the center strand, thus making it the center strand. Bring the right-hand side of the T over the new center strand. Continue in this manner, left strip over center, right strip over center. Pull each strand after each motion to keep the tension even and the braid firm. The folded edges should not show on the top or the bottom of the braid. Try to keep them to the right so they face inside.

205

FOUR-STRAND BRAID

To make the four-strand braid it is necessary to start with two vertical strips in the center of the horizontal top of the T. Start from the left and bring strand 1 over 2, under strand 3, and over strand 4, the right hand extension of the T. Repeat, always starting from the left with braid 1 over 2, under 3, over 4. In the same way 5 strands can also be braided. Thinner strips are recommended for braids of 5 or more strands. Six strands should be started in two sets of three strands each. As soon as the two individual sets of three strands are started, place them close together, flat on a board, and arrange the strands in order for weaving them 1 over 2, under 3, over 4, under 5, and over 6.

Starting four strands

ROUND TURN/ROUND RUG

The round turn is the clue to keeping a braided rug flat on the curves. Start a round rug by bringing the left strand over the center strand twice in succession, then use the right strand, pulling up the right strand tightly. Continue braiding the first left-hand strand twice to each single turn of the right-hand strand until the diameter of the circle is at least 3″, then start regular braiding. As the round rug increases in size, less allowance for rounding is needed.

Braiding four strands

OVAL RUG

The length of the center braid to a great extent determines the proportion of the oval rug. The most pleasant oval is only slightly longer than it is wider. If you were to plan a 9′ × 12′ oval, you would begin with a straight center braid about 3′ long before starting to work around it. The sections on each side of the center braid would be approximately 4½′ wide. A 4′ × 6′ rug might start with a 2′ straight center braid, and smaller rugs could begin with a 1′ center braid. There is no set formula for making a specific size of rug because braid sizes vary. Anything less than a 1′ center is likely to become a circle rather than an oval. After braiding the center length, use the round turn at both ends

Making a round turn

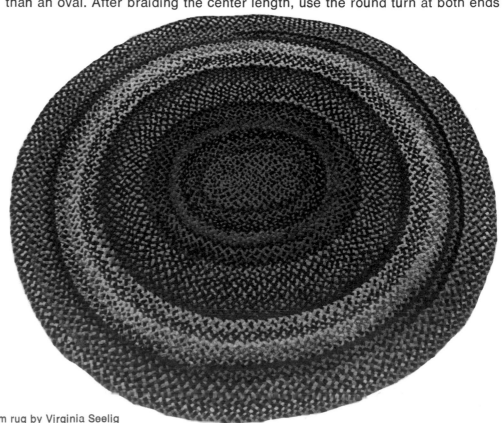

Braided oval dining-room rug by Virginia Seelig

to keep the rug flat.

Braid down the straight length, starting to lace the braids together almost immediately so as to place the round turn correctly. The round turn may be needed for several rounds or until the curve is expanded.

SQUARE AND RECTANGULAR RUGS

The sharp right-angle turn of a square requires that the left-hand strip make two turns around the center strip before the right-hand strip is braided around the center one. Pull the right-hand strip tightly to pull up the corner. Start with a suitable length of braid, remembering that the center length determines the size and shape of the rug because each braid will go completely around the starting strip. Make two sharp corners and continue braiding back to the beginning of the center length. Lace the two pieces together. Set the needle and thread aside (there is no need to cut the thread) and make the third and fourth corner. There may be one or two regular braid turns between the short corners, depending upon the weight of the material. Continue making the corner turns when needed.

Turning a right angle

LACING THE BRAIDS TOGETHER

If the needle is sharp, file the point down until it is blunt enough to pass beneath the loops of the braid without picking up any of the material. To begin lacing after a reasonable amount of braiding has been finished, place the work on a flat surface and lay the braid in place. Use heavy cotton or linen thread, such as warping thread or shoemaker's thread. A circle will require that the center be sewn together in order to keep the end in place and the initial coils going around tightly before starting the lacing. Always keep the side being laced near you and the bulk of the work on the far side. Be sure to lace from the same side each time. Expert braiders consider it easier to lace from the same side as that on which the work was braided. However, you may choose to lace with the face down because the folded edges on the opposite surface may have been more carefully controlled during braiding. Braided rugs are meant to be reversible, so all lacing must be invisible. Alternate braiding and lacing in short lengths make it much easier to keep the rug flat, and the corners will turn more readily. Start with a knot, hiding it under a fold. Draw the thread under the inside loop of the braid, working back and forth from one to the other, between the two edges. Draw the thread very tightly so that no thread is visible between loops. Usually no loops are skipped, but occasionally it is necessary to skip alternate loops on curves to ease in the fullness. Before the thread ends, attach a new length with a square knot. Pin the braid on the curves in a trial run to estimate the amount of extra outside loops needed to round the curve as the size increases. Place a pile of books on the rug to hold it on the table as you are braiding. If any cupping occurs, correct it immediately by unlacing some of the braiding and carefully pinning the strip and releasing the tension before relacing. Rippling occurs when the work is too loose. Sometimes holding a steam iron over a bulge will help settle it back into place. A wet towel with a weight over it will help to reduce the bulge by slightly shrinking the fabric braids.

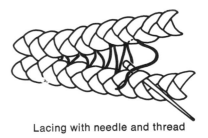

Lacing with needle and thread

TAPERING TO FINISH THE ENDS

When the desired size has been reached, remove the Braid-Aids if they have been used, and taper the ends of the strips to slim them, starting back about 6″ and cutting on the diagonal. The Braid-Aids can be replaced to finish the turning under, but it is just as easy to fold in the raw ends and sew them to-

Tapering off

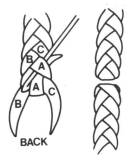

Butting braid ends

gether. After sewing, braid them a bit farther, lace, then insert the ends into the adjoining braid, pulling the ends through with a crochet hook. Stitch them to the braid invisibly to secure.

BUTTING ENDS

Contemporary braiders designing for contemporary interiors may wish to devise dramatic new arrangements. Patchwork squares, awning strips, checkerboard patterns, diamonds, or blocks of triangles are all possible. Bright color schemes, sharp contrasts, such as black and white, need sharp endings for distinct color changes. The ends can be finished flush or squared off and butted together. First taper the ends after the last braid, sewing the folds together, then pull them back into the braid with a crochet hook one at a time. Do not cut off any protruding ends; tuck them under until the braid is smoothly finished. If it is necessary to trim the ends, sew them down for added security. Butt two ends and carefully sew through the ends until they are invisibly joined.

Design for a braided rug

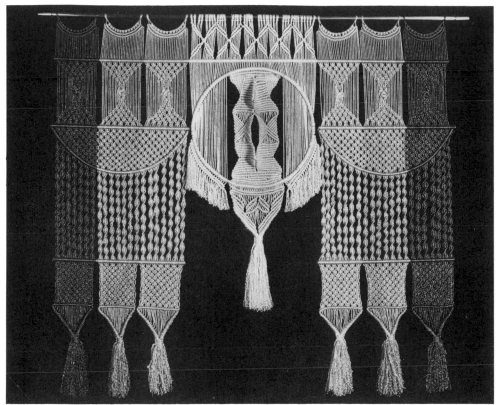

Wall hanging of hand-dyed silk in four shades of green by
Moonyeen McNeilage. Collection Mrs. S. Philips. Photo John
Amiet

MACRAME

IF ANY METHOD OF CONSTRUCTION needs no equipment, that method is macramé. Apart from needing the necessary fibers, something to lean upon, a few T-pins, and the knowledge of one or two knots, anyone is set to begin anywhere, anytime. Like all other very sensible, practical forms, macramé's antecedents go back to a distant time when it must be supposed that very sensible, practical people, having found a need and a way to tie a knot, then perceived the rhythmic beauty of knots made in series. Macramé is, after all, no more than square knots (another name for the sailor's reef knot) and half hitches tied horizontally, vertically, and diagonally. Other descriptive or fanciful names are only variations on these basic knots. Decorative knotting, or macramé, is said to have originated with the Arabs and spread through Europe after the Moors introduced the technique to Spain. Elaborate fringes with long tassels were widely used as finishes for woven cloth, as valances on four-poster beds, and as lacy additions to clothing, especially during the Victorian era. Practical knotters produce a variety of useful items, including belts, bags, table mats, rugs, and the increasingly popular plant hangers. As a medium for wall hangings and rugs, macramé's potential is inestimable. It is supple, easy to maneuver and manipulate, and can be worked flat or in the round in any weight of fiber. Size is not limited to the dimensions of a frame or loom. Color is a matter of choice.

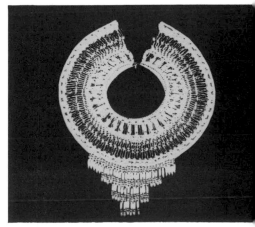

Macramé collar by Cornelia Reina

MATERIALS

Large pieces can be worked on a table, on the floor, or suspended from a bar or hanger of any kind. A padded clipboard or cork board is a more comfortable support for small pieces worked sitting down at a desk, in the lap, or at a table. The soft surface is necessary for the T-pins or stick pins that hold the work.

A tremendous variety of materials are recognized today as adaptable and effective for knotting rugs, wall hangings, and sculpture. Jute is one of the most satisfactory fibers from the points of view of economy and thickness. Its

209

natural color is soft and attractive, it can be dyed, and it is available in many finishes, from smooth to rough. At the other end of the scale, braided white nylon parachute cord, probably the most expensive fiber, is as luxurious as it is beautiful. Try to purchase silky parachute cord in surplus supply shops that may carry rejected reels of irregular cordage, or seconds. The irregularities do not affect the sturdiness of the cord, and undesirable sections can be cut away.

Cotton cable cord, seine twine, linen, and some wools are excellent for knotting. Almost any type of cord found in marine supply stores has the added advantage of being able to withstand weather and dampness. Waxed whipping cord is a favorite among people making necklaces and other types of jewelry because it makes a tight, clearly defined knot, and threads easily through small beads. About the only unsuitable yarns are those with too much elasticity, such as knitting yarn.

Artist-craftsmen working in macramé often use materials that are difficult to handle and not very durable but that provide broad-scale and interesting textural effects. Cotton-covered welting cord is available in diameters of more than 1″ from upholstery supply houses. Unspun roving and handspun yarns are extremely interesting when combined with other types of fiber. Sisal, although hard on the hands, takes dye with a jewel-like quality. Copper wire, metallic thread, and opaque or clear plastic tubing add a different dimension when used judiciously. The effect of light on slender clear tubing knotted in the round or cascading from a wall hanging is surprisingly ethereal in effect.

Macramé planter of cotton cord with interior glass container. American, c. 1890. Collection of the author

GLOSSARY

OVERHAND KNOT
A knot formed by bringing one end of a cord through the center of a loop formed in the cord

HOLDING CORD/KNOT BEARER
A length of cord around which knots are formed

T-PIN
Long, sturdy, straight pins with a wide crossbar at the top

REVERSE DOUBLE HALF HITCH (LARK'S HEAD)
Doubled-over cord forming a pair of loops around another cord or a dowel

ENDS
Length or section of cord selected and arranged for working

FILLER CORDS
Vertical or horizontal cords supplying a core for knots

HALF KNOT
Half of a square knot

SQUARE KNOT
The basic knot of macramé, made with two ends tied in two stages around two or more filler cords

HORIZONTAL DOUBLE HALF HITCH (CLOVE HITCH)
A single cord looped twice around a separate horizontal cord

VERTICAL DOUBLE HALF HITCH
A single vertical cord looped twice around another vertical cord

DIAGONAL DOUBLE HALF HITCH
A single cord looped twice around a cord held diagonally

Macramé knotting is generally prepared by setting up any number of ends (lengths of cord or yarn) that is divisible by two or four on the board, bar, or holding cord. Designs that include a predominance of square knots would make a number of ends divisible by four a preferable beginning. Rugs and wall hangings may be fringed on one side, on both sides, or may remain totally without fringe. Decide where you want the fringes to be before cutting the ends of cord. A flush finish (one without fringe) is started with reversed double half hitches (lark's heads) set up by doubling over single cords to make two ends. When a fringe is desired on both ends of a rug, begin with cut ends, tying each pair in an overhand knot three or more inches away from the cut end of the cord. Fix each pair to a knotting board, pushing a T-pin through the center of the overhand knot. Draw a horizontal line across the board in order to place the overhand knots evenly and closely together. After a firm heading of horizontal double half hitches the loose ends will be secured.

Approximately eight times the desired finished length of the piece will be used up in knotting. Thick fibers will take up more yarn in each knot than thin fibers. Measure the lengths generously. Working cords will always come to an end faster than inert core or filler cords. Whenever a piece is started with rows of horizontal double half hitches (or double half hitches made in any direction) allow the right- or left-hand cord to be many times longer than all other cords. Double half hitches are always worked around a bearer cord, and it is convenient to have this cord as long as possible. However, it is impractical to use extremely long cords because they fray and unply with excessive handling. Long cords should be tied up to a workable length in butterflies. In the case of thick fibers, such as jute, wind it around your fingers and secure the loop with a rubber band. A great deal of yardage would be necessary for a bearer cord used in making a rug composed entirely of double half hitches. The bulky bundle of tied-up cord would prove cumbersome. As you work, renew the ends of reasonably long lengths by splicing before they become too short to handle. Lay a new cord alongside an end about 6″ long, continuing to knot until the new cord is secure, then drop the short end behind the work. Filler cords for square knots are replaced in the same way. After completion of the piece, cut or work the short ends into the body of the fabric with a crochet hook.

HOLDING CORDS, RODS, AND DOWELS

A fringeless beginning requires a method for holding the knotting cords. Consider the purpose of the piece before you start. Most items of apparel and utilitarian use require a soft edge. With the exception of belts (which can be started directly on the buckle) the holding cord usually should match the body of the work in color and weight. Wall hangings can be started on a dowel, a round or square plastic rod, a branch, or a length of metal that will serve the multiple purpose of holding cord, heading, and hanging device. In the case of a light-weight wall hanging, a matching bar can be worked into the knotting just before the piece is finished, to weight the hanging at the bottom.

OVERHAND KNOT AND HOLDING CORD

Decide the width of the piece to be knotted. Cut a generous width of cord to hold the knots. Place the overhand knots at either side, pinning them securely to the knotting board with T-pins. Extensive lengths beyond the overhand knots may be needed as knot-bearing cords for double half hitches. These knot-bearing cords can be incorporated with the filler cords of the square knots at the edges until needed again as knot bearers.

REVERSE DOUBLE HALF HITCHES (LARK'S HEADS)

Reversed double half hitches are used for mounting the knotting cords or the holding cord or rod. Ends are always doubled over before mounting begins. Hold the end with the loop down behind the holding cord and insert the two cut ends through the loop from front to back. If the loop is drawn up and over the holding cord and the ends are inserted from back to front, the knot is the same but provides a different effect. This difference may add a desired variety to the design, particularly when cords are added in the center of the work to make increases in width. Keep the holding cord horizontal during mounting.

HALF KNOT

The half knot is one half of the formation known as the square knot. Two reverse double half hitches or four ends are needed. The two center cords are filler cords and are held taut while the two outside cords are tied around them. Hold the two center filler cords between the third and fourth fingers of the right hand. Bring the left-hand cord across the two center filler cords in a wide swoop. Hold it across the filler cords with the thumb and index finger. Bring the right-hand cord down over the left-hand cord. Push it under the filler cords with the right hand. Pull it through the wide arc of the left-hand cord with the left hand. Tighten the two outside cords around the filler cords. Repeated over and over again, the half knot starts to turn around and around involuntarily. Because of this unique characteristic, the half knot braid is sometimes known as the spiraling sinnet.

SQUARE KNOT

In macramé, the square knot is composed of two half knots tied in two stages around the front and back of two or more filling cords. Prepare the cords for

Overhand knot

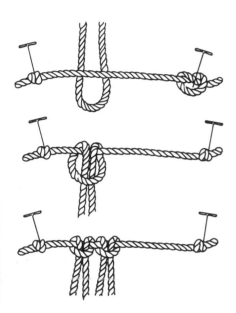

Making a lark's head knot

Half knot

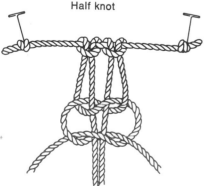

Square knot

knotting in the same way as for the half knot. The first part of the knot is tied by following the directions for tying the half knot. For the second half of the knot, take what is now the left-hand cord in a wide arc behind the filler cords. Bring the right-hand cord straight down behind the left-hand cord. Bring the right-hand cord up over the filler cords and down through the wide arc formed by the left-hand cord from front to back. Holding the two filler cords taut, grasp the two outside cords and tighten the knot.

The square knot can be used as a gathering knot, grouping and holding any number of cords. A firm fabric is formed by alternating the position of the square knots in each row. When each row is started a distance away from the previous one, an open fabric is formed. Place a square knot on each set of four ends all across the row. On the second row, ignore the first and second cords and start the square knotting with the third and fourth cords. At the end of this row two unused cords will remain. Start the third row with the first four cords, knotting all across the row. To alternate or stagger the knots brick fashion, ignore the first two and the last two cords in every other row. Symmetrical pieces can usually be worked from either the left or the right side. However, working consistently from left to right eliminates confusion when starting or stopping work.

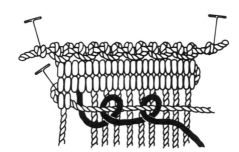

Making a horizontal double half hitch

Continuing rows of horizontal double half hitches

HORIZONTAL DOUBLE HALF HITCHES

In this knot the end cord (either the holding cord or the first cord on the left or right) becomes the knot bearer. Hold the knot bearer over all the other cords mounted on the holding cord. The bearer cord must be held taut and higher than horizontal in order to keep the rows flush with one another. Each cord emerges in succession from under the knot bearer and is looped twice around the knot bearer with the end brought through the loop each time, forming the double half hitch. It is advisable to start all half hitch headings with horizontal double half hitches to ensure a straight edge.

Making a vertical double half hitch

VERTICAL DOUBLE HALF HITCHES

Each mounted cord becomes a knot bearer in vertical double half hitches. Starting from left to right, the end cord is the knotting cord. Place it underneath the next vertical cord. The knotting cord always comes from behind the knot bearer, loops around it with the cord end being carried up behind the vertical cord and through the loop. Make two half hitches, then move to the next vertical knot bearer. The knotting cord is carried behind the entire row of vertical cords. When the right-hand side is reached, place a T-pin on the board to maintain a straight edge and bring the knotting cord around it in preparation for the return to the left-hand side. Do not attempt to place more than one double half hitch on each vertical cord. Add another set of half hitches on the return row. Push upward and tighten each set of half hitches. An entire piece worked in vertical double half hitches is somewhat impractical because they have a tendency to slip downward. Vary rows of vertical double half hitches with rows of horizontal half hitches.

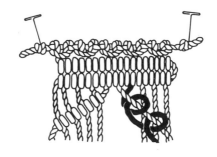

Vertical double half hitch with horizontal heading

DIAGONAL DOUBLE HALF HITCHES

Diagonal double half hitches are worked on a knot-bearing cord in the same way as the horizontal double half hitches. The difference is in the angle of the knot-bearer cord. The degree of the angle is a matter of choice. Divide the cords evenly, working from the center toward the outside, or from the outside toward the center, making chevrons or diamonds.

Knotting diagonally

Necklace of half hitches and beads by Cornelia Reina. Photo Charles Reina

THINGS TO NOTE AND REMEMBER:

- Hold the knot-bearing cord taut and motionless.
- To insure tight, level horizontal rows of double half hitches, hold the knot-bearing cord higher than the row above the one in process.
- Mark the position of the hand holding the knot-bearing cord for diagonal half hitches on the board in order to resume the same angle when starting and stopping.
- Tie all knots close to each other unless the design indicates otherwise.
- Keep ends in order, straight and untwisted.
- Cut and eliminate frayed or distressed sections of cord.
- Sear the ends of nylon cord to prevent fraying.
- Stop knotting at least six inches before the end of a cord. Never end a cord on the selvage. Add a new cord before the last three inches of the right- or left-hand side is reached.
- Cut ends of slippery fibers can be held in place with a drop of white glue applied with a toothpick.
- Work all unwanted cut ends back into the fabric with a crochet hook or a blunt yarn needle.
- If blocking is necessary, staple the finished piece to a board, and mist-spray with water. Allow to dry overnight.
- A large rug of heavyweight yarn or jute can be worked from the center outward to eliminate the problem of unwieldy lengths of yarn. This method works best with an all-over design of half hitches. A very comfortable way to work from a sitting position can be arranged by setting up the fibers over a bar suspended from ropes, like a swing. Work the two sides of the design alternately. The weight of the materials provides enough tension.

Detail of diamond-shaped diagonal double half hitches surrounding a square knot worked with double cords

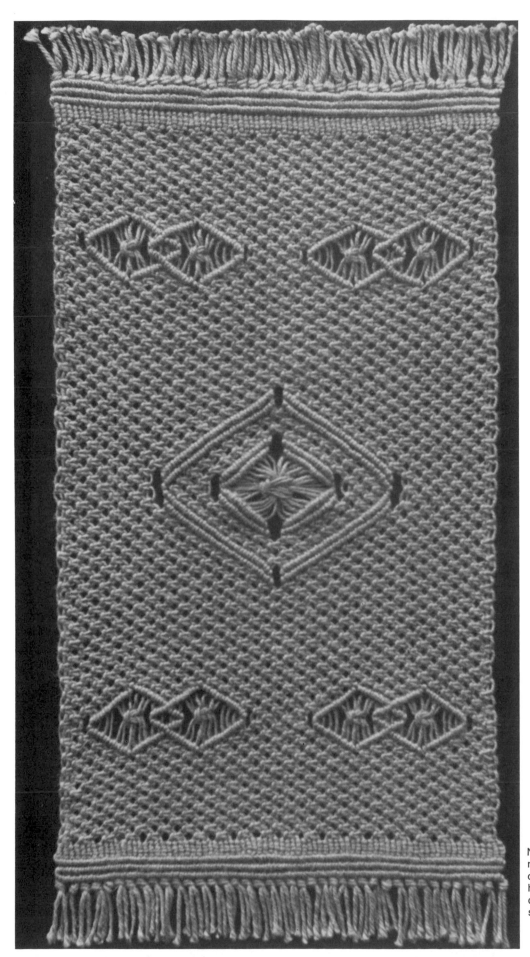

Natural jute macramé rug by Cornelia Reina. Knotted with 2½ balls of #10 three-ply jute twine, using horizontal, vertical, and diagonal double half hitches and alternating square knots

Horizontal bars and vertical rows of double half hitches

Diamond of horizontal double half hitches surrounded by vertical double half hitches

Checkerboard of vertical and horizontal double half hitches

Natural jute macramé rug by Michael Cornfeld, a sampler of horizontal and vertical double half-hitch design patterns. The rug is worked in three one-foot strips, each strip composed of five different designs. The three strips were laced together with heavy linen warping thread.

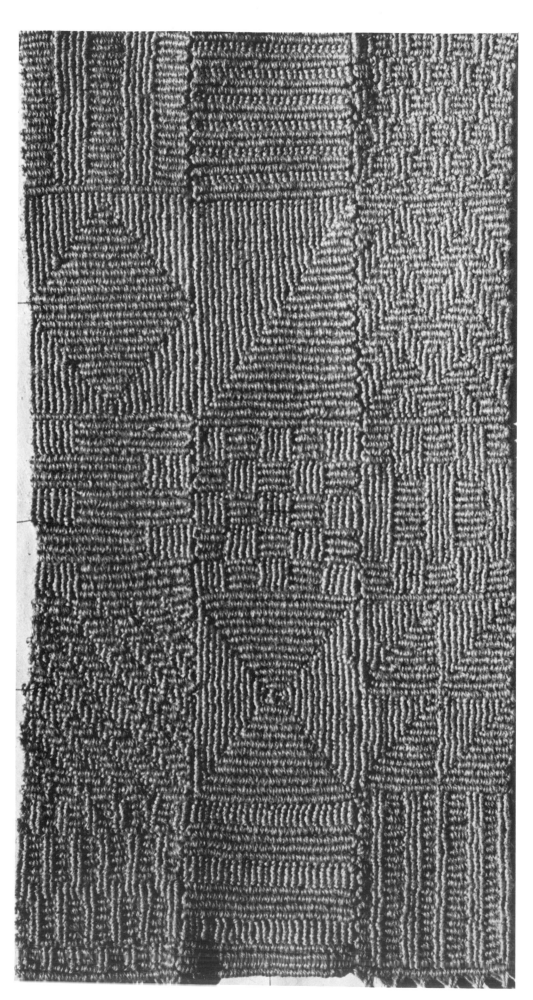

216

Stop and Go pattern

Short alternating verticals and horizontals

Two by Two pattern

Double triangles

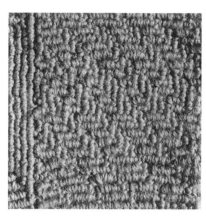

Diagonal zigzags

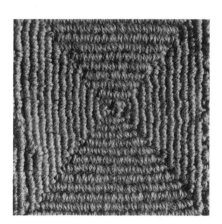

Four triangles

Horizontal stripes

Square chain

Zigzag of horizontal and vertical double half hitches

Basket weave

Small triangles

Ladder Stitch

217

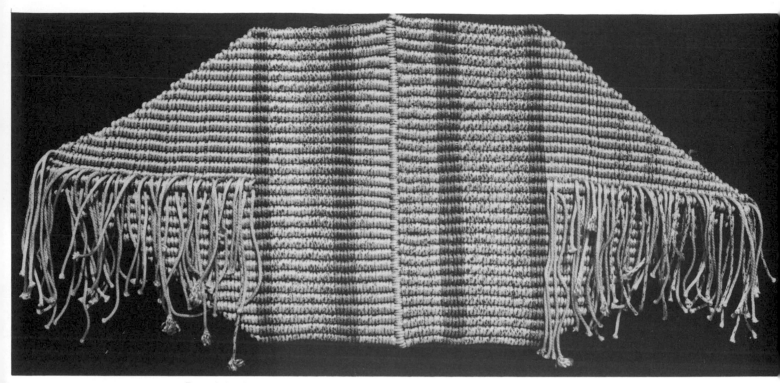

Rug of dyed-nylon parachute cord by Jan Silberstein worked from the center outward

Comet by Aurelia Muñoz. Detail of suspended three-dimensional sculpture

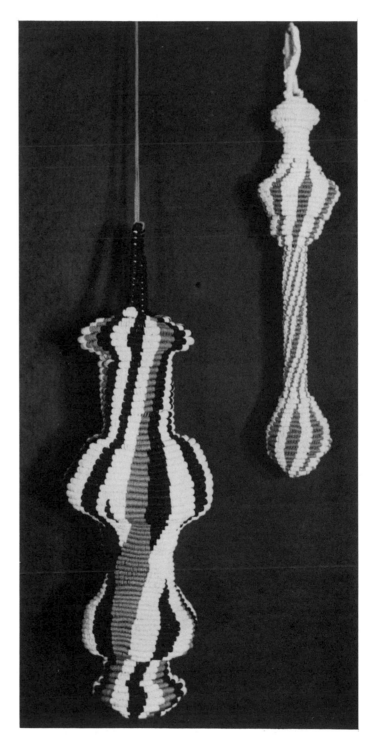

Sculptured wall hanging of Ghiordes
knots and macramé by the author

Many of the suppliers here are mail-order firms; others are wholesale distributors who will sell to schools or in large quantities. Ask the wholesale distributors for information and the location of the nearest dealers. Request price lists, catalogues, color charts, samples, and shipping charges. There often is a charge for samples and catalogues. Most suppliers' samples are a worth-while investment.

SUPPLIERS

YARN

Craft Yarns of Rhode Island, Inc. (rug wool, homespun, linen)
603 Mineral Springs Avenue, P.O. Box 385, Pawtucket, Rhode Island 02862, U.S.A.

The Mannings (rug wool, general supplies)
East Berlin, Pennsylvania 17316, U.S.A.

Lily Mills
Shelby, North Carolina 28150 U.S.A.

Paternayan Brothers, Inc. (rug wool, monk's cloth, Duraback)
312 East 95th Street, New York, New York 10028, U.S.A.

My Mother's Warp (rug wool, wool winders, cordage)
434 West 14th Street, Huntington, West Virginia 25704, U.S.A.

Cooper-Kenworthy, Inc. (rug wool, novelty yarn, jute)
564 Eddy Street, Providence, Rhode Island 02903, U.S.A.

Mexiskein (Mexican homespun yarn)
P.O. Box 1624, Missoula, Montana 59801, U.S.A.

Creative Yarns (wholesale rug wool)
Box 507, Louisa, Kentucky 41230, U.S.A.

The Yarn Depot, Inc. (rug wool, cotton, novelty yarns)
545 Sutter Street, San Francisco, California 94102, U.S.A.

J. Hyslop Bathgate and Co. (wool, novelty yarn)
Island Street, Galashiels, Scotland

William Condon and Sons, Ltd. (wool)
65 Queen Street, P.O. Box 129, Charlottetown, Prince Edward Island, Canada

CUM Textile Industries (rug wool, cowhair, linen)
5 Rosemersgade 1362, Copenhagen K, Denmark

Borgs of Lund (wool, cowhair, linen)
P.O. Box 96, Lund, Sweden

Stravros Kouyoumoutzakis (natural rough-spun wool)
Kalokerinov Avenue 166, Iraklion, Crete, Greece

Rammagerdin
Hafnar Straeti 5 & 17, Reykjavik, Iceland

Briggs and Little's Woolen Mills, Ltd. (wool)
York Mills, Harvey Station, New Brunswick, Canada

UNSPUN WOOL

Greentree Ranch (fleece, spindles, homespun)
Route 3, Box 461, Loveland, Colorado 80537, U.S.A.

Golden Fleece Woolens (fleece)
Box 123, Agincourt, Ontario, Canada

LINEN

Frederick J. Fawcett, Inc.
129 South Street, Boston, Massachusetts 02111, U.S.A.

SCANDINAVIAN YARN AND WOVEN BACKING

Coulter Studios, Inc.
138 East 60th Street, New York, New York 10022, U.S.A.

House of Kleen (imported wool, cowhair, rug backing)
P.O. Box 224, North Stonington, Connecticut 06359, U.S.A.

NAVAJO WEAVING EQUIPMENT (HAND-HEWN TOOLS BY NAVAJO TOOLMAKERS)

Living Designs
    313 South Murphy Avenue, Sunnyvale, California 94086, U.S.A.

RUG HOOKING SUPPLIES

George Wells, The Ruggery (Paternayan yarn, rug-backing accessories)
    565 Cedar Swamp Road, Glen Head, New York 11545, U.S.A.

Rittermere Crafts Studio Ltd.
    P.O. Box 240, Vineland, Ontario, Canada

Wilson Brothers Mfg. Co. (Tru-Gyde Needle)
    Route 8, Box 33H, Springfield, Missouri 65804, U.S.A.

Rug Crafters (Speed Tufter/Montell Hooker; wool, other equipment)
    3895 South Main, Santa Ana, California 92704, U.S.A.

Yarn Painter Electric Hooker
    P.O. Box 4564, Fresno, California 93744, U.S.A.

Norden Products (hookers)
    P.O. Box 1, Glenview, Illinois 60025, U.S.A.

Columbia-Minerva Corp. (hookers)
    295 Fifth Avenue, New York, New York 10016, U.S.A.

CORDAGE

Ludlow Corporation, Textile Division (jute)
    Needham Heights, Massachusetts 02194, U.S.A.

Seaboard Twine and Cordage Co., Inc. (jute)
    49 Murray Street, New York, New York 10007, U.S.A.

P. C. Herwig Co. (macramé cord)
    264 Clinton Street, Brooklyn, New York 11201, U.S.A.

George B. Carpenter & Co.
    401 North Ogden Avenue, Chicago, Illinois 60622, U.S.A.

AAA Cordage Co.
    3238 North Clark Street, Chicago, Illinois 60657, U.S.A.

CLOTH CUTTERS, BRAIDING EQUIPMENT

Harry M. Fraser Company
    192 Hartford Road, Manchester, Connecticut 06040, U.S.A.

KNITTING NEEDLES, CROCHET HOOKS, RUG HOOKING EQUIPMENT

C. J. Bates & Son, Inc. (Susan Bates products)
    Chester, Connecticut 06412, U.S.A.

The Boye Needle Co.
    4335 North Ravenswood Avenue, Chicago, Illinois 60613, *or* 195 Bonhomme, Hackensack, New Jersey 07601, U.S.A.

J. P. Coates, Ltd.
    155 St. Vincent Street, Glasgow, Scotland

GENERAL ART AND CRAFT SUPPLIES

J. L. Hammett Co.
    Hammett Place, Braintree, Massachusetts 02184, U.S.A.

Dryad Handicrafts
    Northgates, Leicester, England

School Products, Inc. (weaving equipment)
    312 East 23rd Street, New York, New York 10010, U.S.A.

BIBLIOG-RAPHY

Abbey, Barbara. *The Complete Book of Knitting.* New York: The Viking Press, 1971; London: Thames and Hudson, Ltd., 1972

Allard, Mary. *Rugmaking: Techniques and Design.* Philadelphia: Chilton Book Company, 1963

Bennett, Noel, and Bighorse, Tiana. *Working with the Wool.* Flagstaff, Arizona: Northland Press, 1971

Beutlich, Tadek. *The Technique of Woven Tapestry.* New York: Watson-Guptill Publications, 1971

Christie, Mrs. Archibald. *Samplers and Stitches.* London: B. T. Batsford, Ltd., 1920; Great Neck, New York: Hearthside Press, Inc., 1971

Collingwood, Peter. *The Techniques of Rug Weaving.* London: Faber and Faber, Ltd., 1968; New York: Watson-Guptill Publications, 1971

D'Harcourt, Raoul. *Textiles of Ancient Peru and Their Techniques.* Seattle: University of Washington Press, 1962

de Dillmont, Therese. *Encyclopedia of Needlework.* Mulhouse, France: D.M.C. Library; in United States, distributed by Joan Toggitt, Ltd., New York

Emery, Irene. *The Primary Structures of Fabrics.* Washington, D.C.: The Textile Museum, 1966

Harvey, Virginia I. *Macramé, the Art of Creative Knotting.* New York and London: Reinhold Publishing Corp., 1967, 1968

Harvey, Virginia I., and Tidball, Harriet. *Weft Twining Shuttle Craft Guild Monograph #28.* Pacific Grove, California: Craft and Hobby Book Service (Select Books), 1969

Hawley, Walter A. *Oriental Rugs Antique and Modern.* New York and London: Dover Publications, Inc., 1970

Kahlenberg, Mary Hunt, and Berlant, Anthony. *The Navajo Blanket.* New York: Praeger Publishers, Inc., in association with the Los Angeles County Museum of Art, 1972

Kent, William Winthrop. *The Hooked Rug.* New York: Tudor Publishing Co., 1937

————. *Rare Hooked Rugs.* Massachusetts: Pond Ekberg Co., 1941

Landreau, Anthony N., and Pickering, W. R. *From the Bosporus to Samarkand: Flat Woven Rugs.* Washington, D.C.: The Textile Museum, 1969

Lesch, Alma. *Vegetable Dyeing.* New York: Watson-Guptill Publications, 1970

Marein, Shirley. *Stitchery, Needlepoint, Appliqué and Patchwork.* New York: The Viking Press, 1974; London: Studio Vista, Ltd., 1974

Meilach, Dona Z. *Macramé: Creative Design in Knotting.* New York: Crown Publishers, 1971; London: Allen & Unwin, Ltd., 1971

Philips, Mary Walker. *Step-by-Step Knitting.* New York: Golden Press, 1967

Tattersall, C. E. C. *Notes on Carpet Knotting and Weaving.* London: Victoria and Albert Museum, 1961

Tidball, Harriet. *Contemporary Tapestry Shuttle Craft Guild Monograph #12.* California: Craft and Hobby Book Service, 1964

Wiseman, Ann. *Rag Tapestries and Wool Mosaics.* New York and London: Van Nostrand Reinhold Co., 1969

————. *Islamic Carpets.* New York: The Metropolitan Museum of Art Bulletin, June 1970

INDEX